M000074197

Inklings on Philosophy, Theology, & Worldview

INVITED TO TRUST

UPDATED 4TH EDITION

WP Wheaton Press
Train. Equip. Reflect.

Philosophy, Theology, & Worldview
Updated and Expanded 4th Edition
Student Leaders Guide

© 2017 by Matthew Dominguez
© 2014, 2015, 2016 by Matthew Dominguez
Published by Wheaton Press
Wheaton, Illinois
www.WheatonPress.com

All rights reserved. No part of this publication may be reproduced, stored in a retrieval system, or transmitted in any form or by any means-for example, electronic, photocopy, recording-without the prior written permission of the publisher. The only exception is brief quotations in printed reviews.

ISBN-13: 978-0692227213 (WheatonPress.com)
ISBN-10: 0692227210

1. Christian Education – Discipleship 2. Spiritual Formation – Discipleship. 3. Life of Christ – Education.
4. Nonfiction-Religion and Spirituality-Christian Life. 5. Nonfiction-Spiritual Growth-Christ-centered.

Copyright and Trademark Standard

The Reflect Assessment™ copyright 1996, 2004, 2010, 2017 Wheaton Press™. All Rights Reserved. Free to download, copy, distribute, repost, reprint and share, for non-commercial use provided it appears in its entirety without alteration with copyright information and WheatonPress.com both visible and unaltered.

Scripture quotations are from The Holy Bible, English Standard Version® (ESV®), copyright 2001 by Crossway, a publishing ministry of Good News Publishers. Used by permission. All rights reserved.
Scripture taken from the Holy Bible, NEW INTERNATIONAL VERSION®.
Copyright 1973, 1978, 1984 by Biblica, Inc.
Scripture taken from The Holy Bible: International Standard Version (ISV),
Copyright 1998, 2008. All rights reserved.
Scripture quotations are taken from the Holy Bible, New Living Translation, copyright ©1996, 2004, 2007. Used by permission of Tyndale House Publishers, Inc., Carol Stream, Illinois 60188. All Rights Reserved.
New American Standard Bible Copyright © 1960, 1962, 1963, 1968, 1971, 1972, 1973, 1975, 1977, 1995 by The Lockman Foundation, La Habra, Calif. All rights reserved.
Scripture taken from the Contemporary English Version®
Copyright © 1995 American Bible Society. All rights reserved.
GOD'S WORD® is a copyrighted work of God's Word to the Nation. Quotations are used by permission. Copyright 1995 by God's Word to the Nations. All rights reserved.

This document contains proprietary research, copyrighted materials, and literary property of Wheaton Press™, Engaged Schools™ and Examine™ are all trademarks of Wheaton Press™. All other trademarks noted are property of their respective owners.

Accordingly, international and domestic laws and penalties guaranteeing patent, copyright, trademark, and trade secret protection safeguard the ideas, concepts, and recommendations related within this document.

Syllabus
Structure
Logistics &
Expectations

Philosophy & Theology
INVITED TO TRUST

"See to it that no one takes you captive through hollow and deceptive *philosophy*, which depends on human tradition and the elemental spiritual forces of this world rather than on

CHRIST"

Colossians 2:8

"Always be prepare to give an answer for the hope that you have, but do this with *Gentleness and Respect*"

I Peter 3:15

 ©2010, 2017. Wheaton Press™ All Rights Reserved.

Table of Contents

Shakespeare, Journey, and The Invitation to Joy

Notes on the Shakespearian structure

The material and scope and sequence of this course and thus this book lends itself to be broken into different scenes in a personal story. I have taught Shakespeare for 15 years and I love how he structures his plays. I intentionally chose to artistically and stylistically structure this book in the context of a Shakespearian play. Of course the themes and focus if this book lends itself to a smoothly dove tail with many of the Bard's sentiments. I have chosen to honor the request of my students who have asked me to keep this brief explanation in the introduction. Firstly, as I have already mentioned, I want your interaction with this Thinkbook to feel like a journey of sorts, like you are in a play as one of the characters, undergoing the feelings and struggles that a character on stage might be working through. Shakespeare is a master story teller and a master at character development. What he can do in the span of three to four hours is remarkable. Additionally, I chose this structure so that reading this book could be like experiencing play, were after putting it down you are left with something to contemplate and process. One of the beauties of a Shakespearian play is that we have been doing just that for 400 years, and for so many of us, each time we walk away we are left with an indelible mark on our minds, hearts, and even our souls.

One of the approaches to understanding the five act Shakespearian structure is to look at how he sets up each act. Although there is variance and nuance, as we analyze some of the key elements offered to the viewer in each act we can see why he does what he does when he does it. I have attempted to do the same here. In Act 1 he presents the setting, characters, and main themes. I tell my students that watching a Shakespearian play is like walking into a themed party. You will catch the theme of the party, be it a birthday, a Hawaiian luau, a graduation party, or even a celebration of a life before of after a funeral. At the start of the Party you will be introduced to the main characters and you will get to know why you are there and what the party is about. Act two is where he offers the Plot, Subplot, and a few more key characters. He saves the plot and subplot - the main tensions – of the play for act two most likely because if he offers it in act one we will miss it due to our efforts of simply trying to figure out what is going on, and why you are there. The tensions of a story are what make a story a story worth watching or listening to. Our lives our filled with tension! We love stories because the best stories and the best authors help us find sufficient and satisfying resolution to the tensions in our own unfolding stories. In act three Shakespeare will help us to start finding clarity, we will see the climax of the tensions peak, and we will be offered a retelling of the tale, just in case we are lost. Interestingly many people give up on a great story, especially Shakespeare, before hitting the climax and gaining clarity because of feeling confused or overwhelmed by the tensions and the interplay of the characters as that story unfolds... the same could easily ring true for a book of philosophy and world view. For a Shakespearian play, unlike may tales and novels, the story does not start the slow decent into resolution after act three. In Act four Shakespeare will bring in the unexpected twist or two or three, he will ratchet the tensions even higher creating intrigue, mystery, and delve deeper into the tension and themes! He will take the plot into the stratosphere, which is risky for a story if you cannot bring it back to earth in a meaningful way and in the space allotted with a short drama on stage. Fortunately, Shakespeare can and does help his readers and viewers land the story! This is why so many writers have adopted his style as a template. In Act five he will offer resolution to the tensions in the play that are authentic and real, there will be great catharsis, and he always leave us thinking, chewing, processing, and pondering as we walk out of the performance or put the text down. If you have this in mind as you think through the material presented in this book, it may help you understand why I chosen to place each scene where it is. I hope you enjoy this book like your favorite movie or play that you come back to it time and again for new connections or use it to share in meaningful thoughtful conversations...

 ©2010, 2017. Wheaton Press™ All Rights Reserved.

Shakespeare, Journey, and The Invitation to Joy

Notes on the Shakespearian structure

At the foot of the cross on which Christ hung, the soldiers who crucified him divvied up his clothes "into four parts, one part for each soldier; also his tunic. But the tunic was seamless, woven in one piece from top to bottom, so they said to one another, 'Let us not tear it, but cast lots for it to see whose it shall be.' This was to fulfill the Scripture which says, 'They divided my garments among them, and for my clothing they cast lots.'"

In chapter 3 of his book Orthodoxy, G.K. Chesterton poignantly points out that we have "torn the soul of Christ into silly strips." We have ripped apart the fullness of reality—Christ Himself—and held onto a piece of the Truth as if it is the whole.

I have taught philosophy to high school students in a Christian setting for many years now. As I have shared with them the four major worldviews in which we humans trust, I have come back again and again to this quote by Chesterton. And as I teach my students that each worldview is but a portion of the Truth—though we trust in the one we hold to as if it were the whole—I am convinced more and more deeply that the fullness of Truth and reality are found only in the undivided person of Christ.

In this book, I write in the same way that I teach. I take heady philosophy and break it down for high school students. Because I am also a lover and teacher of literature, as I mentioned on the previous page, this book is organized in acts, with these acts following a plot line of sorts and finishing with a climax.

In Act I, I will discuss the common denominator of trust. No matter what "ism" we follow, we are trusting in something. Everything is based on trust. The only way humans live is to make decisions based on whatever we consider trustworthy, though we differ on the object in which we place our confidence. We give authority to whom and what we trust, and it is essential for us to understand that every decision we make is based on our conclusions regarding the nature of reality.

In Act II, we will look at the "ism"s we trust in: Chesterton's "silly strips." Using the metaphors of a cloth stripped into pieces and an art masterpiece cut into sections, we will examine the fractured realities that result. Idealism, Materialism, Dualism, and Theism each hold a portion of the Truth, yet none has the full reality. I am neither endeavoring to exalt any one of these above another, nor setting them up only to knock them down. I want to highlight and honor the portion of Truth each one holds.

Act III puts the "strips" back together and examines Christ as the fullness of reality. I invite readers into a full way of seeing everything—in the person of Christ. The Truth from each of the four "ism"s is put together, seamlessly, in Him. In Him we find both complete Truth and Grace.

Act IV examines the paradoxes of Christ, for paradox is the only way to make sense of what we encounter in the world. This requires mystery and wonder. It requires embracing the paradox—and, paradoxically, finding resolution.

Act V looks at how trust in the person of Christ alone leads us into paradoxical living. We must be concerned with the nitty-gritty of life—how we do every small thing—and yet we must also be fully immersed in our lives as part of a great, true story. When we truly believe that this Story encompasses every person, we will be compelled to do everything in love and honor.

My greatest goal for this book is that it points its readers to the person of Christ. This book is not Truth; it is simply a mirror for discovering your own object of trust and a map that will help you find the Real Truth, whom you can trust with full confidence. "You shall know reality, and that shall make you free." If this book gets you close to the living, resurrected person of Christ—who will change your life—it will have done its job.

©2010, 2017. Wheaton Press™ All Rights Reserved.   7

Class Overview

Essential Questions

1. What do I believe?
2. Why do I believe it?
3. What difference will my beliefs make in my life?

Unit Essential Questions

Act 1
(Unit 1)   What is really real?

Act 2
(Unit 2)   What are the four main worldviews?

Acts 3
(Unit 3)   What is the Fullness of Reality? Why is Paradox essential for the fullness of reality?

Act 4
(Unit 4)   What is a Christ-centered incarnational worldview? What is the fullness of Christ?

Act 5
(Unit 5)   What is your quest in relation to The Quest?

Course Description

This course combines the study of the basic philosophy and Christ-centered theology with the exploration of the highly influential works of G.K. Chesterton, C.S. Lewis, and J.R.R. Tolkien, including *Orthodoxy*, *Mere Christianity*, *The Great Divorce*, and selections from *The Silmarillion*, *The Hobbit*, and *Lord of the Rings*. Students also study original works from world-renowned philosophers such as Plato and Nietzsche. Class discussion is centered on becoming a "real Christian" and choosing to make one's faith personal, dynamic, active, and joy-filled.

Key Outcomes

1. Students will develop a deep awareness and understanding of the doctrines of justification, sanctification, and imputation in the context of a Christ-centered worldview and in contrast to other philosophical worldviews.

2. Students will examine the four major metaphors for salvation and gain a deeper appreciation for the grace of God.

3. Students will develop a worldview with a clear Christ-centered mission statement that guides them in the fulfillment of God's purposes through their lives.

   ©2010, 2017. Wheaton Press™ All Rights Reserved.

Learning Goals

1. Students will strengthen their faith and increase their joy and understanding within their personal relationship with Christ.

2. Students will differentiate between the four basic views of philosophy and answer seven foundational questions of philosophy for each worldview.

3. Students will examine evidence that will build their confidence in why choosing to believe and follow Jesus is the best choice through the examination and comparison of contrasting worldviews.

4. Students will gain a general historical background on the lives of Lewis and Tolkien.

5. Students will understand the fundamental beliefs of Platonic and neo-Platonic philosophy.

6. Students will broaden their scope of understanding on interpreting various types of literature through literary technique and worldview systems.

7. Students will gain a broader and deeper understanding of humanity and the implications of being both materially human and spiritually eternal.

Learning Skills

1. Students will improve literacy skills, aiming for excellence in communication through reading, creative writing, research, and technical writing.

2. Students will utilize and refine tools such as writing, studying, thinking, discussing, presenting, and communicating theologically, which will help develop competence and confidence in articulating a distinctly Christ-centered worldview through philosophical, theological, and biblical lenses.

Students should come with an open heart and mind. They should be willing to ask questions, discuss answers, and gain new perspectives. Students should come with the expectation to dive in and use their intellect and imagination.

Course Purposes

1. To help students strengthen their faith and increase their joy and understanding in their personal relationship with Christ

2. To discuss *how* and *why* we believe in Jesus and follow His way (especially in contrast to the other numerous, insufficient ways available to humanity)

3. To provide students with general biographies of Tolkien and Lewis

4. To help students understand the fundamentals of Platonic and neo-Platonic philosophy, including a description of the "Shadowlands"

5. To guide students in a deeper understanding of several of the Inkling's spiritual concepts. Topics include, but are not limited to:
   - Being "real"
   - Reality of the spiritual
   - Being "God-bearers"
   - Temptation and sin
   - Living "in joy"
   - Heaven and hell
   - Free will
   - Personal rights
   - Consequences of sin
   - The nature of evil
   - The Power of Paradox
   - Perichoresis
   - Our "journey"
   - Rationality, irrationality, and a-rationality
   - Absolutes/ relativity/ universal Truth
   - Christian myth ("The true myth")

Photo courtesy of Prince Joel Swick

6. To broaden one's scope of understanding and interpretation of literature:
   Topics include, but are not limited to:
   - Brief history of a vision (dream), poem, and novel
   - Symbolism, metaphor, allegory, applicability
   - Imagination and reason
   - Myth, mythopoeic literature, and fantasy literature
   - Apologetics and philology

7. To strengthen students' ability to read, appreciate, and analyze literature

8. To gain a deeper appreciation for the power and beauty of symbolic and metaphoric language

9. To improve literacy skills, aiming for excellence in communication through reading, creative writing, research, technical writing, and rewriting

10. To appreciate and perceive the wondrous world around us more richly

11. To help gain a broader and deeper understanding of humanity and what it means to be mortally human yet spiritually eternal

12. To embrace the invitation into a life giving authentic relationship with Christ

 ©2010, 2017. Wheaton Press™ All Rights Reserved.

What to Expect

Through the duration of this course, students will:

- Participate in journaling and in-class discussion, expressing their understanding of the readings, films, discussions, and various spiritual topics
- Read and show understanding through discussion on several handouts and texts including *Orthodoxy*, *Lord of the Rings*, *Mere Christianity*, *The Last Battle*, and *The Great Divorce*
- Participate in small group presentations on characters/chapters in *Lord of the Rings* and *The Great Divorce*
- Express verbally and in writing their personal understanding of Platonic philosophy, Shadowlands, Christian myth, and various other theological and philosophical topics that arise during the course
- Create a researched, scholarly article on one aspect of the Inklings
- Watch and discuss the films *The Fellowship of the Ring*, *The Two Towers*, *The Return of the King*, and *Shadowlands*
- Critically analyze texts, scripts, films, and interpretations through small and large group discussion, written assignments, and creative activities
- Read passages aloud for the class
- Participate in written and verbal dialogue with academic scholarship and criticism about the Inklings
- Complete creative projects connected to topics associated with the Inklings
- Explore/utilize personal spiritual application of insights gained from the novels

Author	Text	Pagination Notations
Chesterton	*Orthodoxy*	Required – Available online
Lewis	*Mere Christianity*	Required – Available online
Lewis	*The Great Divorce*	Recommended not required
Lewis	*The Last Battle*	Recommended not required
Tolkien	*The Fellowship of the Ring*	OPTIONAL

Notes on Class Structure
Some issues to discuss

- ❑ Homework/Reading:
    - "Philosophy": A key goal of this course is to introduce you to these influential authors and teach you how to read these books
    - Expectations: Read, annotate, and respond (NO summaries!)
    - Policy:

- ❑ Cell Phone and Computer Use:
    - "Neutral tool"
    - "Declaration"
    - "The gentle nudge"
    - Tweets, Instagram, Snapchat, Facebook

Philosophy & Theology General Course Outline (Ending With Tolkien)

Overview	Day 1	Day 2	Day 3	Day 4
Week 1	Intro… LOTR video 4 Circles. Philo "Hammer"	Sillibus and Code Intro & "World Of Worldviews"	"Thy Kingdom Come…" Syllabus and Code Video "Inception" & General Concepts	"Faith Island" & "Chair" Introduce Trust List Concept & *Ephesians*
Week 2	Allegory of the Cave	Discussion on Cave "Coming out of the Cave"	Pre-Assessment: Philo "Quiz" Overview of the 4 Main Trust Lists (Four Circles)	Intro To Idealism
Week 3	Discussion of Idealism & Notes: Words of the Buddha…	Idealism Notes Idealism Videos "7 Years in Tibet" - *Philippians*	Intro to Materialism & Notes	Materialism More Notes: Video "Emperors Club"
Week 4	Materialism "Frankenstein" & "Dark Knight" & Chesterton Orthodoxy Ch. 3 "Suicide of Thought"	Materialism Nietzsche "Mad Man"	Dominguez Story time and 5$ bill Poem - *Ecclesiastes*	Intro To Monism & Notes
Week 5	Monism: "Star Wars" & "Avatar" & "The Last Samurai"	Monism Notes & Story about Brother Ben	*Brother Ben Story! Journey, Not Neutral, Testing the Spirits…*	Crazy Arm Thing and Discussion… - *1 John* Miracle - Testimonies
Week 6	Discussion on Relativity… Discussion on Testing the Spirits…	Intro to Religious Theism Theism Notes and Differentiation - *John* *"Distinction & Ego"*	Religious Theism	More discussion on Religious Theism Islam/Judaism/Deism
Week 7	Wrap up "Philo" Explain Real Grace and that Grace is only a Yahweh Thing…	Discussion on Perfection… *Galatians*	MIDTERM ON A BLOCK DAY & Mid-Assessment: Philo "Quiz" – (Are you learning? Doing Better?)	C.S. Lewis Video "The Magic Never Ends" & General Biography…
Week 8	Mere Christianity Book I Discussion… *Romans*	Mere Christianity Book I Discussion…	Wrap Up MC with "Bono & U2" "With or Without You"	Chesterton Orthodoxy Ch. 6: "Paradoxes of Christianity"
Week 9	MC Book II: "Math" & "Lord Liar Lunatic" & "Sin is Warped Good"	MC Book II: "How it Works" & "Why Jesus"	MC Book II: "Free Will Parfait"	"Truman Show": Pursue truth discussion: What are you willing to do? - "Seek and Ye Shall Find"
Week 10	"The Last Supper" and the "Silly Strips" A Trinitarian Christ Centered World View! Chandelier, Paradox, & Perichoresis…	"This is not a Pipe!" Act 4 of Inklings Book: "The Means to the End" & The Mary Magdalene Hug. LOVE! Intimacy. Lord of the Dance	The Last Battle Chapter 3: Aslan and Tash and the Little Sheep… False Prophecy and False Prophets!	The Last Battle Ch. 15: Emeth.& Dwarves at the End. The Greatest of these is LOVE! And the Goal is intimacy with God!
Week 11	*Introduce FELLOWSHIP Test! "Lesson on Idealism"*	The Great Divorce: Discussion on how to read… "The Three Doors" Invitation to Joy and Intimacy.	GD Ch 1-3 "Quiz" and "how to read the book" *James*	GD Ch 4: "Big Ghost" & "Apostate"
Week 12	GD Ch 5-9 "Shame Girl"	GD Ch 5-9 "Lizard Man" & Killing Sin! *1 Corinthians*	GD Ch 10-13 (Love) "Hilda", "Pam", "Sarah Smith & Tragedian"	GD Ch 14 The Ending and "Lewis" (Wrap Up)
Week 13	ACTS TEST!	BIG Grace Discussion	Test Review and Discussion	Tolkien Bio Video. Tolkien MYTH! *Colossians*
Week 14	Tolkien What is Lit? Tolkien Myth video	The Great Myths and The True Great Myth! Quotes on Myth from Workbook…	*Set up the Final: Introduce the Concept of Life as Epic Journey and Adventure – "Follow Me"*	Tolkien Silmarillion with Audio and Full discussion
Week 15	Hobbit! With Audio	Hobbit Discussion – Riddles in the Dark – Paradoxes to save your life!	Hobbit conclusion and LOTR Character Discussion *Acts*	LOTR Character and Plot. Start "The Quest" and Maps
Week 16	FOTR "Quest": Shire – Old Forest	FOTR "Quest": Bombadill - Bree	FOTR "Quest": Weathertop - Rivendell	FOTR "Quest": Moria & Balrogs Part 1
Week 17 FINALS	FOTR "Quest" Lorien – Breaking of Fellowship	FOTR "Quest": Fall Of Borimir	ROTK: "Destruction of the Ring!" "Eagles…"	FINAL: Post-Assessment: Philo "Quiz" Share time and Turn in Journey and Quest!

 ©2010, 2017. Wheaton Press™ All Rights Reserved.

Learning Assignments, Readings, and Projects

Philosophy, Theology, and Worldview Assignments

Formative Assessments ("Homework"):

Introduction to the Course:

- Community Core Values of Love and Honor: Read, annotate, and sign in workbook
- "Reflect Assessment": Read, highlight, and discuss in workbook
- William Brown, World Of Worldviews: Read, annotate, and create a typed Analytical Reader Response
- Plato, Allegory of the Cave: Read, annotate, and type out two questions for class discussion
- Philip Yancey, "Prophet Of Mirth: Read, annotate, and create a typed Analytical Reader Response
- Chesterton, Orthodoxy, Ch. 1: Read, annotate, and create a typed Analytical Reader Response

Christian Theism and Theology:

- Chesterton, Orthodoxy, Ch. 3 "Suicide of Thought": Read, annotate, and create a typed Analytical Reader Response
- Chesterton, Orthodoxy, Ch. 4 "Ethics of Efland": Read, annotate, and create a typed Analytical Reader Response
- Chesterton, Orthodoxy, Ch. 6 "Paradoxes of Christianity": Read, annotate, and create a typed Analytical Reader Response
- C. S. Lewis, Mere Christianity, Book I: Read, annotate, and create a typed Analytical Reader Response
- C. S. Lewis, Mere Christianity, Book II : Read, annotate, and create a typed Analytical Reader Response
- C. S. Lewis, Great Divorce, Ch. 1-3: "Quiz" (Notes on "How to Read")
- C. S. Lewis, Great Divorce, Ch. 4-13: Character Profile in workbook: Ghost
- C. S. Lewis, Great Divorce, Ch. 4-13: Character Profile in workbook: Solid Character
- C. S. Lewis, The Screwtape Letters, Ch. 4: Read, annotate, and create a typed Analytical Reader Response
- C. S. Lewis, The Screwtape Letters, Ch. 13: Read, annotate, and create a typed Analytical Reader Response
- C. S. Lewis, The Screwtape Letters, Ch. 26: Read, annotate, and create a typed Analytical Reader Response
- C. S. Lewis, The Last Battle, Ch. 1-4: Read, annotate, and create a typed Analytical Reader Response
- C. S. Lewis, The Last Battle, Ch. 5-11: Read, annotate, and create a typed Analytical Reader Response
- C. S. Lewis, The Last Battle, Ch. 12-16: Read, annotate, and create a typed Analytical Reader Response

The True Myth Life as Epic Journey:

- J. R. R. Tolkien, Silmarillion (The Opening two Chapters): Read, annotate, and complete workbook response
- J. R. R. Tolkien, The Hobbit Ch 5; "Riddles in the Dark": Read, annotate, and complete workbook response

Scripture Reading Assignments:

Ephesians: Faith Island, The Trust List, The Cave: Read, annotate, and complete Written Response
Philippians: Idealism: Read, annotate, and complete Written Response
Ecclesiastes: Materialism: Read, annotate, and complete Written Response
I John: Monism: Read, annotate, and complete Written Response
John: Theism: Read, annotate, and complete Written Response
Romans: Mere Christianity, Book I: Read, annotate, and complete Written Response
Galatians: Mere Christianity, Book 2: Read, annotate, and complete Written Response
James: The Great Divorce: Read, annotate, and complete Written Response
I Corinthians: Silmarillion, Opening Chapters: Read, annotate, and complete Written Response
Colossians: The Hobbit: "Riddle in the dark": Read, annotate, and complete Written Response
Acts: The Fellowship of the Ring: Read, annotate, and complete Written Response

Summative Assessments:

Pre and Post Assessment: Philosophy Objective Information Quiz (fill in the blank)
Midterm: Philosophy and Mere Christianity Creative Celebration of Gifts Project
Objective Information Quiz: Book of Acts (50 point objective quiz)
        Lesson on Grace with response on class blog
Final Exam: "Quest" assignment and "Character Connection" written analysis piece

Expectations

Describe your favorite and most effective learning environment. Give three concrete examples (things we could do during this learning experience) of what worked well.

- This definitely helped me learn:

- This definitely helped me learn:

Describe your worst and most ineffective learning environment. Give three concrete examples (things we should not do during this learning experience) of what did not work well.

- This definitely did not helped me learn:

- This definitely did not helped me learn:

Describe your ideal learning environment. Give three learning environment dreams (things we should not do during this learning experience to help your dreams come true). What just might work?

- This might help me learn:

- This might help me learn:

Goals

"The more I put into this class, the more I will get out of it."

Describe at least five of your personal goals for this class. Why did you sign up for it? What do you hope to learn? Be sure to create some goals if you have not thought of any before today.

- I

- I

Describe your personal expectations for this class. Ask yourself, "What will I be disappointed in if we did not talk about this by the end of this course?" (These are topics you hope we discuss, questions you hope we address, or experiences you hope we have together.)

- I

- I

 ©2010, 2017. Wheaton Press™ All Rights Reserved.

Developing a Kingdom Mindset of Love and Honor

Philosophy & Theology

INVITED TO TRUST

Devotional Thought
"Thy Kingdom Come": A prayer for this course and this class

Matthew 6:9-13

9 Pray then like this: "Our Father in heaven, hallowed be your name.

10 Your kingdom come, your will be done, on earth as it is in heaven.

11 Give us this day our daily bread,

12 and forgive us our debts, as we also have forgiven our debtors.

13 And lead us not into temptation, but deliver us from evil.

Devotional Thought

"Open Our Eyes So We Can See"
The core story and prayer for this curriculum

2 Kings 6:15-17

When the servant of the man of God rose early in the morning and went out, behold, an army with horses and chariots was all around the city. And the servant said, "Alas, my master! What shall we do?" He said, "Do not be afraid, for those who are with us are more than those who are with them." Then Elisha prayed and said, "O LORD, please open his eyes that he may see." So the LORD opened the eyes of the young man, and he saw, and behold, the mountain was full of horses and chariots of fire all around Elisha.

 ©2010, 2017. Wheaton Press™ All Rights Reserved.

"A New Command I Give You, Love…"

Love: The "most excellent way" for everybody to grow on adventures in learning

"Love is patient, love is kind. It does not envy, it does not boast, it is not proud. It is not rude, it is not self-seeking, it is not easily angered, it keeps no record of wrongs. Love does not delight in evil but rejoices with the truth. It always protects, always trusts, always hopes, always perseveres." I Corinthians 13:4-7

Why is this important for an adventurous learning and living environment?

What would this look like in our class? On any adventure experience?

Thoughts to Consider. Prayerfully write the following next to the list below.

I am…

God is…

Patient

Kind

Not envious

Not boastful

Not proud

Not dishonoring to others

Not self-seeking

Not easily angered

Keeping no record of wrongs/ forgiving

Not delighting in evil but rejoicing with truth

Protecting

Trusting

Hopeful

Persevering

Community Core Values of Love and Honor

Each member of this class (including the teacher) is expected to be a positive active learner during this course. The following pages are foundational elements for developing a thriving community of learning, and each member of this class is expected to use these values to contribute in developing a healthy, vibrant community of learners. If you do not understand how to contribute in the following ways, please ask someone to help you find understanding and motivation. Also, please pray for this class as we will be growing closer to the Lord and seeking greater understanding of His Living Word. This is a front-line class! Are you ready to fight? Are you ready to love? We must work together when we are furthering his kingdom come!

Think of these principles as the "backbone" and support; you and the students in your particular classroom will make up the life blood, flesh, and personal quality of the story. You need to create your own set of sturdy ribs from these principles which will in turn protect the vital organs of yourself, your fellow students, and your guests in the "body" of your classroom.

A key part of this time is to help answer some essential questions, such as: What does an effective community look like? How will we make this work? What's the atmosphere in the room or group? We want to create a kingdom environment that is saturated with honor, love, safety encouragement, grace, joy, acceptance, courtesy, and respect.

The main objective of this exercise to collaboratively develop a document of "Core Values and Key Guidelines" that the entire group has created together. Ultimately, every member (starting with the teacher/leader) of the group needs to metaphorically and literally sign their name to the final document.

7 Core Values to Consider:
Love, Safety, Respect, Honor, Community, Learning and Fun

The community code is like a math problem:

IF we are loving and safe
+ (and) we give respect and show honor
+ (and) we intentionally build community
+ (and) we learn because we were created to love learning
= We will have a loving and fun community.

Expectations are the key to how someone feels about an experience before, during, and after the experience. Some tips to remember about expectations:
- Nobody wants to waste time and energy.
- Everybody wants to stay safe. Nobody wants to get hurt, especially publically.
- Everybody actually wants to learn.
- None of us have any real (full) idea of what the person next to us is going through or has been through in the past. Compassion and grace are essential.
- No community, especially a learning community, should have fear, shame, or unhealthy guilt as motivators. It does not work and is counterproductive.
- Joy, fun, curiosity, wonder, delight, and hope are the most effective learning motivators.

 ©2010, 2017. Wheaton Press™ All Rights Reserved.

Love

"Love is patient, love is kind. It does not envy, it does not boast, it is not proud. It is not rude, it is not self-seeking, it is not easily angered, it keeps no record of wrongs. Love does not delight in evil but rejoices with the truth. It always protects, always trusts, always hopes, always perseveres." 1 Corinthians 13:4-7

Why is love important for a positive learning and living environment?

What would this look like in our class?

Safety

Most people think of merely physical safety. Ironically, not being safe in the other areas tends to create deeper, longer-lasting wounds. The truth is, people will not take risks or be vulnerable if they do not feel safe, even if it is a physically safe environment. If a participant speaks up, tries something new, or shares and is made fun of at all they will probably not attempt this again, and others will be less likely to share in the future.

Physical Safety:

Respect personal boundaries, touching appropriately, etc.
Don't horse around.

Emotional Safety:

No put downs, no put downs, no put downs! (This includes nonverbal put downs too.)
Dress appropriately.
No sarcasm and no "just kidding." If you have to say "just kidding," you have already messed up. We cannot have fun at someone else's expense. (Proverbs 26:18&19)
Build each other up, be sincere, be kind, and show compassion.

Spiritual Safety:

We are all at different places on our epic journeys to know Jesus. Ask yourself, Is this a safe place for someone who does not believe in Jesus? Are we helping or hindering others on their journey?
Love each other.
Read 1 Corinthians 13 and actually live it!

Intellectual Safety:

Is this a place where you will not be hurt for your style of learning and your giftedness?
Respect ideas and questions: we can't afford to shut down the asking of questions!

Social Safety:

No gossip, slander, or defacing inside or outside the classroom about anybody.
Use social media appropriately.
Build each other up!
Be intentionally inclusive and pray for each other!

Respect

Respect is all about value, and value can only be bestowed.

Every human being has eternal value, so there's no excuse for disrespecting anyone. Do unto others as you would have them do unto you.

"You treat something how you value it."

Has someone ever mistreated or disrespected something valuable to you?
Can you respect what others value even if you do not value it?
You may need to ask what others value so as to not mistreat their belongings.
Relationship building affects how we value things (and people).
Communication is key; never assume anything based on appearances.

"You treat people how you value them."

How do we treat our best friends, significant others, parents, siblings, strangers, the poor, or the outcast at school?
Think about the "intrinsic" value of a person. We are loved—created in the image of God.
Who are you to say that someone else is not valuable? The living God of the universe died for all people and dances over them with joy and singing (Zephaniah 3).
Are certain people more valuable than others, or do we value them differently?
If so, why do we value people differently?
It's fine to treat people we love well, but can we quickly devalue others by treating them poorly simply because we do not value them? Are they not valuable too?
What if someone thought you were not valuable?
Maybe you don't feel valuable....Why?
What's the difference between how we feel about ourselves and what our true value is?
What's the difference between how we value someone and therefore treat them, and their true value and therefore how we should treat them?

It does not always matter how we feel about someone. People are valuable and should be treated as so.

For the code: Respect leaders, each other, yourself, each others property, the Lord, school property, other adults, chaperones, everybody, leader decisions, God's creation, animals, your school's reputation, the schedule (be on time), use equipment properly, be tactful with your words, be a good listener, value others and show it!

In conclusion:

You may need to learn how to value things differently and learn how to value people as God values them. Interestingly, what a person says and how someone behaves in regards to respect reveals his or her own character and personal values.

 ©2010, 2017. Wheaton Press™ All Rights Reserved.

Honor

Most occurrences of the word honor in the Old Testament are translations of some form of the word *kabod*. The figurative meaning of *kabod* is "to give weight to someone." To honor someone is to give weight or to grant a person a position of respect or authority in one's life.

While honor is an internal attitude of respect, courtesy, and reverence, it should be accompanied by appropriate attention, action, or even obedience; honor without such action is incomplete. - Sam Hamstra, Jr.

Honor is important because...

- It is the glue of a class. It's what builds unity and connection.
- People are powerful and have free will.
- We are un-punishable.
- We need to have a shame-free environment.
- We can call people into their true identity and self.
- Because we want His kingdom to come—here on Earth as it is in heaven.

"Scripture is clear that we have two options—we can choose either to protect the rules and create a religious culture, or to protect our relationships and create a culture of love. And only one of these options is the covenant that Christ died to make with us" (pg. 90).

"When Jesus went to the cross and gave His life as the perfect sacrifice, He… introduced an entirely different reality based on an entirely different relationship between God and mankind. He removed the need for punishment. He removed fear from our relationship with Him. Through the cross, Jesus introduced something into the world that we still don't understand. He has made each and every one of us un-punishable." (pg. 80).

"One of the most vital core values for creating a safe place where people can be free is honor. Honor is the relational tool that protects the value that people have for those who are different than they are… Free people cannot live together without honor… We must be able to be ourselves in this life and community together."
                    - *Culture of Honor*, Danny Silk, Destiny Image, 2009

Community

We need to get to know people outside of our sphere of friends.
No racial digs, gender devaluing, or family degrading.
Look for the good in others and be encouraging.
Be real, open, vulnerable, trustworthy, and honest.
Reconcile and seek community with those you have hurt, intentionally or unintentionally, and always be ready to forgive.
Be polite and courteous.
Get involved. Pray and worship together.

Learning

Learning often takes hard work and will take practice. But it is worth it! It's okay to make a mistake. We often need to make mistakes to grow and learn from them. Learn from past mistakes and others' mistakes. Is this classroom safe enough to make mistakes? How do we make it safe to make mistakes so that we can learn from experience?

We are created differently, but we were all created to love learning! You may not like our education system, but you definitely love to learn and grow! How can we tap into your love for learning and growing?

Don't be afraid to ask for help!

We each have unique learning styles, differences, and paces.

Try new things. Don't be afraid to fail, but learn your limits.

Pay attention, listen, and don't assume that you know everything.

Teach others what you love.

Be willing to be corrected, and be open to change.

Be willing to go deep and share who you are.

Avoid arguments, and instead embrace discussions!

Push yourself.

Actually do the readings and assignments. You have to "practice."

Do devotions; spend time with God, and pray!

Ask the Holy Spirit to help you learn. He is the wonderful Counselor.

Everyone says forgiveness is a lovely idea, until they have something to forgive.
- C. S. Lewis

Artwork public domain

Fun

Set realistic expectations.

There are specific responsibilities for teachers/leaders: Be prepared, read the materials, plan multiple creative activities, etc.

There are specific responsibilities for students: Discussions will be more fun if you have prepared, attitude makes a huge difference, etc.

Students can choose to have an enjoyable class. Whose fault is it if you (teacher and leaders included) are not having fun?

Having fun is a result of specific actions; it is an outcome.

"One's expectations for an experience are directly linked to the quality of that experience for that individual."

If something is not working in class, how do we change that? If you're not learning or feeling safe, think about what the cause is and address it appropriately. I If there is an issue with someone, go directly to the them or the teacher to deal with it.

Have students list how they actually have fun. What is really fun and real fun?

Set a goal to redefine what true fun is. What are some examples of fun in the Bible, and how do these compare to the examples of fun that our secular culture feeds us?

How can we have true joy and the full life that Jesus offers us? After all, Jesus' way of life is the best way to live! But do we really believe this?

Remember that participation is key! It is hard to enjoy an activity if you are not doing it! Furthermore, one's attitude is a choice—you can choose to make an activity fun. You are powerful.

Actively participate in this class its activities and assignments

How can you help our community have fun?

 ©2010, 2017. Wheaton Press™ All Rights Reserved.

Community Code of Love and Honor

We, the participants of this class, agree to abide by and support the following guidelines as members of this community of learners. We also understand that we have discussed and developed these guidelines together so that together we might achieve an environment that is suitable for growing, sharing, having fun, and learning. One main goal of our class is to create a learning environment that is saturated with encouragement, joy, acceptance, courtesy and respect. Upon signing this contract, we are agreeing to put forth effort and cooperation towards the goal of creating a positive and effective classroom community. We understand that humans love to learn and that learning can and should be fun!

I agree to not participate in the following as they do not help create a healthy learning atmosphere.
I agree:
To not be distracting (by using technology, talking inappropriately, or displaying any behavior that inhibits the learning of others)
To not talk while others are sharing or leading
To not put anybody down—even if they are not in our class or as a joke
To not be disrespectful to anybody—particularly with one's body language

I will do my best:
To love and honor others—to be kind and courteous. I believe love is: "The most excellent way to learn as a body of believers."
Therefore in this class, with Christ enabling me, I agree to love others to the best of my ability. I will be patient. I will be kind. I will not envy. I will not boast. I will not be proud. I will not be rude. I will not be self-seeking. I will not be easily angered. I will keep no record of wrongs. I will not delight in evil. I will rejoice with the truth. I will protect. I will trust. I will hope. I will persevere.
To encourage, accept, and help others, and to be inclusive.
To be prepared, individually and as a group participant, and to do my share of my group's work.
To be polite (respecting authority, being quiet, not talking out, etc.).
To "practice what I preach" and "think of the consequences before I speak."
To respect and value others and myself, both emotionally and spiritually.
To be a good listener—actively participating in discussions and sharing.
To work hard and complete assignments, and to strive for excellence for Christ.
To respect each other's and school property.
To help create a safe learning environment:
> Physically (protect the dignity and "temple" of other people; no throwing, poking, pushing)
> Intellectually (respect ideas and learning abilities; no monopolizing discussions)
> Emotionally (be sensitive, supportive, and kind; no laughing at others)
> Spiritually (be loving toward others and their views; spread grace)
> Socially (build others up; no gossiping or devaluing anyone's identity)
To initiate reconciliation with others and the class when I break the code.
To freely offer grace, forgiveness, compassion and acceptance.
To actively and positively participate in class activities and assignments, understanding the more I put into this class, the more I will get out of it!

I have read the above contract. I wholeheartedly agree with it, and I will follow it to the best of my abilities:

Date: _____ Class: ____ Signed: _____

©2010, 2017. Wheaton Press™ All Rights Reserved.

24   ©2010, 2017. Wheaton Press™ All Rights Reserved.

Examíne ™

SPIRITUAL FORMATION TOOL

ChristCenteredDiscipleship.com

"Everyone ought to examine themselves before
they eat of the bread and drink from the cup."
1 Corinthians 11:28

Wheaton Press
Train. Equip. Reflect.

Where are you?

Read. Respond. Reflect.

Directions: *Read through the verses below and highlight or underline any words or phrases that seem to reflect or resonate with where you are at.*

Skeptic. Presented with the person of Christ and the gospel multiple times, I demonstrate disinterest or unbelief.

"Even after Jesus had performed so many signs in their presence, they still would not believe in him." John 12:37, NIV

Characteristics: Calloused heart, dull ears, closed eyes.

"[F]or this people's heart has grown callous, their ears are dull of hearing, they have closed their eyes." Matthew 13:15a, WEB

Christ's Next-Step Invitation: Repent. Believe.

"Then he began to denounce the cities in which most of his mighty works had been done, because they didn't repent." Matthew 11:20 ,WEB

Growth Barrier: A lack of spiritual understanding.

"When anyone hears the message about the kingdom and does not understand it, the evil one comes and snatches away what was sown in their heart. This is the seed sown along the path." Matthew 13:19, NIV

Spiritual Need: A change of mind and heart initiated by the Holy Spirit, a loving and praying friend.

"He said to them, 'This kind can come out by nothing, except by prayer and fasting.'" Mark 9:29, WEB

"As for you, you were dead in your transgressions and sins, in which you used to live when you followed the ways of this world and of the ruler of the kingdom of the air, the spirit who is now at work in those who are disobedient." Ephesians 2:1-2, NIV

Seeker. Questioning, with a desire to learn more about Jesus.

"He answered, 'And who is he, sir? Tell me, so that I may believe in him.'" John 9:36, ISV

Characteristics: A ready heart, open ears, questions with an interest to learn more about Jesus.

"Again, the next day, John was standing with two of his disciples, and he looked at Jesus as he walked, and said, 'Behold, the Lamb of God!' The two disciples heard him speak, and they followed Jesus. Jesus turned, and saw them following, and said to them, 'What are you looking for?' They said to him, 'Rabbi' (which is to say, being interpreted, Teacher), 'where are you staying?' He said to them, 'Come, and see.' They came and saw where he was staying, and they stayed with him that day. It was about the tenth hour." John 1:35-39, WEB

Christ's Next-Step Invitation: Repent. Believe.

"Now after John was taken into custody, Jesus came into Galilee, preaching the Good News of God's Kingdom, and saying, 'The time is fulfilled, and God's Kingdom is at hand! Repent, and believe in the Good News.'" Mark 1:14-15, WEB

Growth Barrier: A lack of clear presentation and understanding of the gospel, a lack of invitation.

"How, then, can people call on someone they have not believed? And how can they believe in someone they have not heard about? And how can they hear without someone preaching?" Romans 10:14, ISV

Spiritual Need: A clear gospel presentation and an invitation to believe and receive salvation.

"But to all who did receive him, who believed in his name, he gave the right to become children of God." John 1:12, ESV

Believer. Presented with the gospel I believe.

"He said, 'Lord, I believe!' and he worshiped him." John 9:38, WEB

Characteristics: Seed begins to germinate, shallow soil, little or no roots.

Other seeds fell on rocky ground, where they did not have much soil, and immediately they sprang up, since they had no depth of soil, but when the sun rose they were scorched. And since they had no root, they withered away. Matthew 13:5-6

Christ's Next-Step Invitation: Follow.

"And he said to them, 'Follow me, and I will make you fishers of men.'" Matthew 4:19, ESV

Growth Barrier: Lack of roots, lack of knowledge, testing, trouble, persecution.

"These in the same way are those who are sown on the rocky places, who, when they have heard the word, immediately receive it with joy. They have no root in themselves, but are short-lived. When oppression or persecution arises because of the word, immediately they stumble. " Mark 4:16-17, WEB

Spiritual Need: Prayer, roots, knowledge, biblical teaching, time, worship and someone to walk with them.

"Like newborn infants, long for the pure spiritual milk, that by it you may grow up into salvation." 1 Peter 2:2, ESV

"So then, just as you received Christ Jesus as Lord, continue to live your lives in him, rooted and built up in him, strengthened in the faith as you were taught, and overflowing with thankfulness." Colossians 2:6-7, NIV

"We continually ask God to fill you with the knowledge of His will through all the wisdom and understanding that the Spirit gives, so that you may live a life worthy of the Lord and please Him in every way: bearing fruit in every good work, growing in the knowledge of God, being strengthened with all power according to His glorious might so that you may have great endurance and patience, and giving joyful thanks to the Father, who has qualified you to share in the inheritance of His holy people in the kingdom of light." Colossians 1:9-12, NIV

The Reflect Assessment™ copyright 1996, 2004, 2010, 2017 Wheaton Press™. All Rights Reserved. Free to download, copy, distribute, repost, reprint and share, for non-commercial use provided it appears in its entirety without alteration with copyright information and WheatonPress.com both visible and unaltered. For more information and complete Scripture, use copyright information available at WheatonPress.com.

Follower. Growing in faith and love; deepening roots and knowledge; struggling with thorns, trials, forgiveness, doubt, and perseverance.

"By this all people will know that you are my disciples, if you have love for one another." John 13:35, ESV

Characteristics: Beginning to push through the soil, struggling with thorns and weeds.

"Others fell among thorns. The thorns grew up and choked them." Matthew 13:7, WEB

"And calling the crowd to him with his disciples, he said to them, 'If anyone would come after me, let him deny himself and take up his cross and follow me.'" Mark 8:34, ESV

Christ's Next-Step Invitation: Deny self; pick up cross; trust, obey, and love Christ and others.

"Then Jesus said to his disciples, "If anyone desires to come after me, let him deny himself, and take up his cross, and follow me." Matthew 16:24, WEB

Growth Barrier: Thorns, worries of this life, doubt, deceitfulness of wealth, comfort, self and self-will.

"Others are those who are sown among the thorns. These are those who have heard the word, and the cares of this age, and the deceitfulness of riches, and the lusts of other things entering in choke the word, and it becomes unfruitful." Mark 4:18-19

Spiritual Need: Deny self; trials; endurance, perseverance, time, small group relationships, and accountability.

"Consider it pure joy, my brothers and sisters, whenever you face trials of many kinds, because you know that the testing of your faith produces perseverance. Let perseverance finish its work so that you may be mature and complete, not lacking anything." James 1:2-4, NIV

"Through him we have also obtained access by faith into this grace in which we stand, and we rejoice in hope of the glory of God. Not only that, but we rejoice in our sufferings, knowing that suffering produces endurance, and endurance produces character, and character produces hope." Romans 5:2-4, ESV

"These have come so that the proven genuineness of your faith—of greater worth than gold, which perishes even though refined by fire—may result in praise, glory and honor when Jesus Christ is revealed." 1 Peter 1:7, NIV

Friend. Marked by obedient love for Christ and others; may wrestle with isolation, complacency and accountability.

"You are my friends if you do what I command you." John 15:14, ESV

Characteristics: Good soil, obedience to Christ, fruit, growing faith, increasing love and perseverance in trials.

"We ought always to thank God for you, brothers and sisters, and rightly so, because your faith is growing more and more, and the love all of you have for one another is increasing. Therefore, among God's churches we boast about your perseverance and faith in all the persecutions and trials you are enduring." 2 Thessalonians 1:3-4, NIV

Christ's Next-Step Invitation: Love, obey, go, teach.

"If you love me, you will keep my commandments." John 14:15, ESV

"Jesus came to them and spoke to them, saying, 'All authority has been given to me in heaven and on earth. Go, and make disciples of all nations, baptizing them in the name of the Father and of the Son and of the Holy Spirit, teaching them to observe all things that I commanded you. Behold, I am with you always, even to the end of the age.' Amen." Matthew 28:18-20

Growth Barrier: Complacency, fear, pride, lack of vision and lack of equipping.

"Then he said to his disciples, 'The harvest indeed is plentiful, but the laborers are few.'" Matthew 9:37, WEB

"How, then, can people call on someone they have not believed? And how can they believe in someone they have not heard about? And how can they hear without someone preaching?" Romans 10:14, ISV

Spiritual Need: Vision, continued obedience, equipping, empowerment, continued spurring and accountability within community.

"…to equip his people for works of service, so that the body of Christ may be built up until we all reach unity in the faith and in the knowledge of the Son of God and become mature, attaining to the whole measure of the fullness of Christ." Eph 4:12-13

"As for you, brothers, do not grow weary in doing good." 2 Thessalonians 3:13, ESV

"Let us continue to hold firmly to the hope that we confess without wavering, for the one who made the promise is faithful. And let us continue to consider how to motivate one another to love and good deeds, not neglecting to meet together, as is the habit of some, but encouraging one another even more as you see the day of the Lord coming nearer." Hebrews 10:23-25, ISV

Fisherman. Reflecting Christ and reproducing fruit of righteousness and good works.

"Because we have heard of your faith in Christ Jesus and of the love you have for all God's people—the faith and love that spring from the hope stored up for you in heaven and about which you have already heard in the true message of the gospel that has come to you. In the same way, the gospel is bearing fruit and growing throughout the whole world—just as it has been doing among you since the day you heard it and truly understood God's grace." Colossians 1:4-6, NIV

Characteristics: Good soil, fruitfulness, harvest, influence, reflecting Christ.

"Others fell on good soil, and yielded fruit: some one hundred times as much, some sixty, and some thirty." Matthew 13:8,

Christ's Next-Step Invitation: Teach others.

"Therefore, as you go, disciple people in all nations, baptizing them in the name of the Father, and the Son, and the Holy Spirit, teaching them to obey everything that I've commanded you." Matthew 28:19-20a, ISV

Growth Barrier: Complacency, fear, pride, lack of vision, lack of equipping, weariness.

"Let's not get tired of doing what is good, for at the right time we will reap a harvest—if we do not give up." Galatians 6:9, ISV

"Think about the one who endured such hostility from sinners, so that you may not become tired and give up." Hebrews 12:3,

Spiritual Need: Perseverance, humility, faithfulness, accountability, reliable people.

"It gave me great joy when some believers came and testified about your faithfulness to the truth, telling how you continue to walk in it." 3 John 3, NIV

"And what you have heard from me in the presence of many witnesses entrust to faithful men who will be able to teach others also." 2 Timothy 2:2, ESV

Examine™: Spiritual Formation Planning Tool
More resources available at WheatonPress.com

Directions: Answer the following seven questions using the words or phrases that you highlighted or underlined.

1. Where am I?

Skeptic. When presented with the gospel, I do not believe.
Seeker. Questioning, with a desire to learn more about Jesus.
Believer. When presented with the gospel, I choose to believe.
Follower. Growing in faith, love, and roots; struggling with thorns, trials, and perseverance.
Friend. Marked by obedient love for Christ and others.
Fisherman. Reflecting Christ and bearing fruit of righteousness and good works.

2. Where would I like to be in six months?

Skeptic. When presented with the gospel, I do not believe.
Seeker. Questioning, with a desire to learn more about Jesus.
Believer. When presented with the gospel, I choose to believe.
Follower. Growing in faith, love, and roots; struggling with thorns, trials, and perseverance.
Friend. Marked by obedient love for Christ and others.
Fisherman. Reflecting Christ and bearing fruit of righteousness and good works.

3. What invitation do I need to respond to in order to take my next step?

Skeptic. Repent.
Seeker. Repent. Believe.
Believer. Follow.
Follower. Deny self. Pick up cross. Obey. Love Christ and others.
Friend. Love. Obey. Go.
Fisherman. Teach others.

4. What barriers will I face?

Skeptic. Calloused heart. Deaf ears. Closed eyes.
Seeker. Lack of clear testimony. Lack of invitation.
Believer. Lack of root. Testing. Trouble. Persecution.
Follower. Thorns. Worries of this life. Deceitfulness of wealth. Comfort. Self.
Friend. Complacency. Fear. Lack of vision. Lack of equipping.
Fisherman. Complacency. Fear. Lack of vision. Lack of equipping. Weariness.

5. What spiritual needs do I have?

Skeptic. Prayer. Repentance. A believing friend.
Seeker. Receive. Believe. Salvation.
Believer. Prayer. Roots. Knowledge. Teaching. Worship. Time.
Follower. Deny self. Trials. Endurance. Perseverance. Time. Relationships and accountability.
Friend. Vision. Continued obedience. Equipping. Opportunity. Empowerment. Accountability within community.
Fisherman. Perseverance. Faithfulness. Reliable people.

6. What steps will I take?

7. Who will I ask to hold me accountable?

The Reflect Assessment™ copyright 1996, 2004, 2010, 2017 Wheaton Press™. All Rights Reserved. Free to download, copy, distribute, repost, reprint and share, for non-commercial use provided it appears in its entirety without alteration with copyright information and WheatonPress.com both visible and unaltered. More information and complete Scripture use copyright information available at WheatonPress.com.

Unit 1
(ACT 1)

Trust, Faith Island, and the Nature of Reality

Philosophy & Theology
INVITED TO TRUST

UNIT 1 (Act 1) ESSENTIAL QUESTIONS:

1. What is the nature of reality?
2. How do humans create a belief system or worldview?
3. What is the suicide of thought? How to get out of it or help others out of it?
4. What is a philosophical axiom?
5. What is the difference between subjective and objective truth?
6. What are the 7 basic questions of reality?
7. What is the nature of reality? What is truly real?

UNIT 1 (Act 1) READINGS:

1. Brown: "World of Worldviews"
2. Plato: *Allegory of the Cave*
3. Phillip Yancey's "Prophet of Mirth"
4. G.K. Chesterton's *Orthodoxy*, Ch. 3 "Suicide of Thought"
5. St. Paul: *Ephesians*

UNIT 1 (Act 1) THINKBOOK LEARNING OPPORTUNITIES:

Formative:

- ❑ *The* "World of Worldviews" Annotations and Reflective Response
- ❑ *The* "Allegory of the Cave" Annotations and Analytical Reader Response
- ❑ "Prophet of Mirth" by Philip Yancey: Annotations and Analytical Reader Response
- ❑ Scripture Reading "Truth Revealed": *Ephesians*
- ❑ "Suicide of Thought" by G.K. Chesterton: Annotations and Analytical Reader Response
- ❑ Trust List: Interview and Friend
- ❑ Trust List: Create Your Own

UNIT 1 (Act 1) LEARNING PLAN:

1. World of Worldviews
2. Discussion on Faith Island and the Trust Lists
3. *Allegory of the Cave*
4. *Prophet of Mirth and Chesterton*
5. Suicide of Thought
6. A look at Philosophical Axioms
7. A look at Subjective and Objective Truths
8. The 7 Basic Questions of Reality
9. The Truman Show

 ©2010, 2017. Wheaton Press™ All Rights Reserved.

"World of Worldviews" By William Brown
Quotes, notes, doodles, and discussion

Here are some reflection opportunities, discussion questions, and quotes to ponder.

1) Meaningless, meaningless: "The World of Worldviews"

> "Would you tell me, please, which way I ought to go from here?" asked Alice.
> "That depends a good deal on where you want to get to," said the Cat.
> "I don't care much where," said Alice.
> "Then it doesn't matter which way you go," said the Cat.
>
> T.S. Eliot: "Teach us to care and not to care..."

2) Worldview: "A comprehensive framework of beliefs that help us to interpret what we see and experience and also gives us direction in the choices that we make as we live out our days" (Richard Wright, 1989).

3) A worldview consists of an explanation, an interpretation of the world, and then an application of that knowledge to life. Today's culture proposes that you should find a worldview that fits you and then live it out. But you shouldn't want a worldview that fits you—you need a worldview that fits the world [reality] and corresponds with truth.

4) Everyone has a story, an explanation of the world—how it came about, why we're here, and what happens when we die. Everyone interprets the world and circumstances through the lens of that worldview.

5) "Religion is the problem." Religion a problem when it is used as an end in itself and not a means to engage in a loving relationship with the Living God of the Universe. Discuss.

©2010, 2017. Wheaton Press™ All Rights Reserved.

Philosophy & Theology

"World of Worldviews" By William Brown
Quotes, notes, doodles, and discussion
More reflection opportunities, discussion questions, and quotes to ponder.

5) "Your worldview is your view both of the world and for the world. You may not live what you profess, but you live what you believe. It's inescapable. We are great at professing, but how we live is rooted in our beliefs. Our worldview is not just a mind-set; it's a "will set."

The Chair Discussion on Faith, Works, and Grace…

6) AMBIGUITY:
"The questions are ultimate because there are answers. What you believe or don't believe is not going to change what happens when you die."

TWO WAYS TO READ THIS LINE:
    a.

    b.

7) "Prepare your minds for action."

"…[Do not conform] any longer to the pattern of this world, but be transformed by the renewing of your mind…"

8) "My strong advice to you is to soak, soak, soak, philosophy and psychology, until you know more of these subjects than ever…"

Fyodor Dostoyevsky (1874) wrote, "Get to know everything so that if [when] you meet a godless man or a man with evil intentions, you can answer him properly, and his wicked and pious words will not befall your young mind."

 ©2010, 2017. Wheaton Press™ All Rights Reserved.

Notes on Faith, Trust, and Belief: "Is Forgiveness Possible?" ER Clip

Find and watch the ER clip with Ryko Alesworth. It is titled "Is Forgiveness Possible? ER".
It is on YOUTUBE: https://www.youtube.com/watch?v=vhxURmVl0IQ.
(It has a man dying of cancer and a hospital Chaplain trying to help him find some peace.)

Here are some reflection opportunities, discussion questions, and quotes to ponder.

"I WANT ANSWERES" – What answers are you Looking for? How about your friends?

I peter 3:15 "Always be prepared to give an answer, But do this with gentleness and respect…" –
What would it take to be prepared for this type of situation – with gentleness and respect.

"Is forgiveness even possible?" – How would you answer this question in this moment?

"I thought an inclusive approach to religion would help?" – Apparently not. Why?

This patient admits that he is afraid of death. Please be sure to note that the Trust List way to do world view is not promoting pluralism and universalism. Using the four world views, which have different consequences and outcomes for what is trusted, come up with at least four different options and their consequences that you can offer the gentleman dying of cancer.

Idealism:

Materialism:

Monism:

Theism:

Other Options:

Learning About Seven Big Philosophical questions in Life:

Views of Reality and Core Philosophy. Although James sire in his landmark book, *The Universe Next Door* 1998, did not invent the popular big questions of philosophy he made them colloquial. I give him due honor credit here for his impact on this text. I have reworked them and reordered them and even added a few of my own.

1. What is the nature of reality: the material or spiritual?

1. Who and what is God?

1. Who is man? What is mankind? What is a human being?

1. What is the basis of and standard for morality?

1. What happens to a human at death?

1. What is the meaning and purpose of human history?

1. Why are we here? Where are we going?

1. What is the purpose of human existence?

Artwork public domain

Field Notes on Faith, Trust, and Belief: Response to the Textbook
The big questions of life

Response to the Text: What would you say to Anna at age 5 as she is holding the lifeless body of her beloved pet? "Papa, where did Pup Go?"

 ©2010, 2017. Wheaton Press™ All Rights Reserved.

Learning Assessment
Interview a friend or neighbor

The Philosophical Trust List of:

Views of reality and core philosophy questions

1. What is the nature of reality: the material or spiritual?

2. Who and what is God?

3. Who is man? What is mankind? What is a human being?

4. What is the basis of and standard for morality?

5. What happens to a human at death?

6. What is the meaning and purpose of human history?

7. Why are we here? Where are we going?

8. What is the purpose of human existence?

Artwork public domain

Learning Assessment
Create your personal Trust List

The Philosophical Trust List of:

Views of reality and core philosophy questions

1. What is the nature of reality: the material or spiritual?

2. Who and what is God?

3. Who is man? What is mankind? What is a human being?

4. What is the basis of and standard for morality?

5. What happens to a human at death?

6. What is the meaning and purpose of human history?

7. Why are we here? Where are we going?

8. What is the purpose of human existence?

Artwork public domain

 ©2010, 2017. Wheaton Press™ All Rights Reserved.

Faith Island and the Trust Lists

The Nature of Reality: Faith Island and the Trust Lists

There are two realms that are a part of every worldview: the spiritual and the material

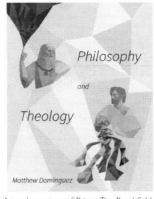

Philosophy

and

Theology

Matthew Dominguez

Artwork courtesy of Prince Tim Burchfield

There are four distinct views to take on how these two realms form reality

IDEALSM   MATERIALSM   MONISM   THESM

◯   ◯   ◯   ◯

(All of the isms, religions, views, tribes, people, and ways are represented within this framework)

"Faith Island"

Key thought for reflection and discussion: Christians can and should believe in absolute objective truth such as God and the Bible. However, a healthy Christian, Muslim, Hindu, or Buddhist will gladly accept and humbly admit that every person's access to God and the Truth presented in their holy texts is through that which is subjective and suspect, such as our perceptions, eyes, emotions, brains, or personalities. (Everything is based on TRUST!)

What are the implications of this reality as we approach what we trust in light of what others choose to trust?

Considering that there are thousands of Christian denominations. What are the denominational implications of this in the body of Christ, the Church as a whole, as Christians all over the planet strive for harmony and unity that Jesus himself prayed for in the Garden of Gethsemane before his death

Inception video clips and discussion
(What are we going to use to figure out this whole reality thing?)

 ©2010, 2017. Wheaton Press™ All Rights Reserved.

Faith Island and the Trust Lists

1. We use what we trust. We give authority to what we trust.

    We use what we trust to formulate our conclusions on the nature of reality. What are you using? What should we be using? What are your classmates using?

    - I Trust
    - I Trust
    - I Trust
    - I Trust
    - I Trust
    - I Trust
    - I Trust
    - I Trust
    - I trust

Photo public domain

"*Always* be prepared…" 1 Peter 3:15

"Faith Island"

Creating a Trust List for the rest of the course…
(What are we going to use to figure out this whole reality thing?)

We need to find that what is trustworthy (worthy of our trust).
What makes something or someone trustworthy?

- We Trust
- We Trust
- We Trust
- We Trust
- We Trust
- We Trust
- We Trust
- We Trust
- We Trust

Key quote: "If objective truth exists—which it most likely does—we must accept that our access to it is through that which is subjective."

©2010, 2017. Wheaton Press™ All Rights Reserved.

Plato's Allegory of the Cave

During the past 2,500 years, few have exerted more influence on the Western thought than Plato (c. 428-348 B.C.). Born into the aristocrat family in the Greek city-state of Athens, Plato received the best education of the day, and he went on to found a school of his own—the Academy—in which he enacted the dialectical model of teaching famously associated with his own teacher, Socrates. Writing in the voice of Socrates, he produced a large number of dialogues (one of which ironically condemns writing) that have shaped Western philosophy, psychology, and politics. These works reveal Plato's literary and rhetorical abilities, inaugurate new forms and use of prose, and set out his theory of the ideal state and a plan for living and learning within it.

Characteristic of many Platonic works is the use of stories featuring extended metaphors and analogies, such as his representation of the human soul as a charioteer trying to manage a chariot drawn by two horses, one docile and obedient, the other unruly and devilish. You can see of these devices at work in "Allegory of the Cave," the climax of Plato's discussion of philosophy in book VII of The Republic, his dialogue about the ideal state.

The story presented in this brief allegory compares the life of people chained in a darkened cave, where they are deluded by shadows, with that of those released into the dazzling sunlight outside. Plato argues that this movement from darkness to light is like the journey the soul must make from the prison of mere sensory impression (appearance or images) to the freedom of true reality, which exists only beyond the realm of the senses. Paradoxically, in Plato's system, what we can see with our eyes is suspect, a mere shadow; only what we can see with our souls is "real."

In making this argument, Plato raises issues as old Western history. What is "real," and what is only apparently real? Which is more valuable, and why? Down through the centuries people have debated these questions, as we are doing in present-day.

From The Presence of Others by Andrea A. Lunsford and John J. Ruzkiewicz

CLASS NOTES ON ALLEGORY OF THE CAVE:

 ©2010, 2017. Wheaton Press™ All Rights Reserved.

Plato's Allegory of the Cave

Analyzing the Text

1. Underline or highlight at least three passages that interest you or that you would like to bring up during group discussion.

1. Write a personal reader response to the passage.

As a good reader the Plot's Allegory of the Cave

is a

1. Create two questions for group discussion and write them below.

Extend Your Learning

4. Working alone or with classmates, read carefully through Plato's allegory of the cave and note all the uses of metaphor, simile, and analogy you can find.

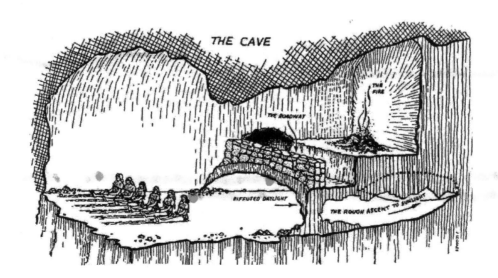

The Cave By Plato:

And now, I said, let me show in a figure how far our nature is enlightened or unenlightened:—Behold! Human beings living in an underground den, which has a mouth open towards the light and reaching all along the den; here they have been from their childhood, and have their legs and necks chained so that they cannot move, and can only see before them, being prevented by the chains from the turning round of their heads. Above and behind them a fire blazing at a distance, and between the fire and the prisoners there is a raised way; and you will see, if you look, a low wall built along the way, like the screen which marionette players have in front of them, over which they show the puppets.

I see. And so you see, I said, men passing along the wall carrying all sorts of vessels, and the statues and figures of animals made of wood and stone and various materials, which appear over the wall? Some of them are talking, others silent.   You have shown me a strange image, and they are strange prisoners. Like ourselves, I replied; and they see only their own shadows, or the shadows of one another, which the fire throws on the opposite wall of the cave?

True, he said; how could they see anything but the shadows if they were never allowed to move their heads? And of the objects which are being carried in like manner they would only see shadows? Yes, he said. And if they were able to converse with one another, would they not suppose that they were naming what was actually before them? Very true. And suppose further that the prison had an echo which came from the other side, would they not be sure to fancy when one of the passers-by spoke that the voice which they heard came from the passing shadow?

No question, he replied. To them, I said, the truth would be literally nothing but the shadows of the images. That is certain.

And now look again, and see what will naturally follow if the prisoners are released and disabused of the error. At first when any of them is liberated and compelled suddenly to stand up and turn his neck round and walk and look towards the light, he will suffer sharp pains; the glare will distress him, and he will be unable to see the realities of which in his former state he had seen the shadows; and then conceive some one saying to him, that what he saw before was an illusion, but that now, when he is approaching nearer to being and his eye turned towards more real existence, he has a clearer vision, —what will be his reply? And you may further imagine that his instructor is pointing to the objects as they pass and requiring him to name them, —will he not be perplexed? Will he not fancy the shadow s which he formerly saw are truer than the objects which are now shown to him? Far Truer

And if he is compelled to look straight at the light, will he not have pain in his eyes which will make him turn away to take refuge in the objects of vision which he can see, and which he will conceive to be in reality clearer than the things which are now being shown to him?

True, he said.

And suppose once more, that he is reluctantly dragged up a steep and rugged ascent, and held fast until he is forced into the presence of the sun himself, is he not likely to be pained and irritated? When he approaches the light his eyes will be dazzled, and he will not be able to see anything at all of what are now called realities. Not all in a moment, he said.

He will require to grow accustomed to the sight of the upper world. And first he will see the shadows best, next the reflections of men and other objects in the water, and then the objects themselves; then he will gaze upon the light of the moon and the stars and the spangled heaven; and he will see the sky and the stars by night better than the sun or the light of the sun by day?

Certainly. Last of all he will be able to see the sun, and not mere reflections of him in the water, but he will see him in his own proper place, and not in another; and he will contemplate him as he is. Certainly. He will then proceed to argue that this is he who gives the season and the years, and is the guardian of all that is in the visible world, and in a certain way the cause of all things which he and his fellows have been accustomed to behold? Clearly, he said, he would first see the sun and then reason about him.

Been in the dark for too long that when sees the right cannot believe it

42   ©2010, 2017. Wheaton Press™ All Rights Reserved.

The Cave By Plato continued:

And when he remembered his first habitation, and the wisdom of the den and his fellow-prisoners, do you not suppose that he would felicitate himself on the change, and pity them? Certainly, he would. And if they were in the habit of conferring honors among themselves on those who were quickest to observe the passing shadows and to remark which of them went before, and which followed after, and which were together; and who were therefore best able to draw conclusions as to the future, do you think that he would care for such honors and glories, or envy the possessors of them? Would he not say with humor,

"Better to be the poor servant of a poor master,"

[handwritten: rather going back to the darkness than stay in the light]

and to endure anything, rather than think as they do and live after their manner? Yes, he said. I think that he would rather suffer anything than entertain these false notions and live in this miserable manner. Imagine once more, I said, such a one coming suddenly out of the sun to be replaced in his old situation; would he not be certain to have his eyes full of darkness? To be sure, he said.

And if there were a contest, and he had to compete in measuring the shadows with the prisoners who had never moved out of the den, while his sight was still weak, and before his eyes had become steady (and the time which would be needed to acquire this new habit of sight might be very considerable) would he not be ridiculous? Men would say of him that up he went and down he came without his eyes; and that it was better not even to think of ascending; and if any one tried to loose another and lead him up to the light, let them only catch the offender, and they would put him to death. No question, he said.

This entire allegory, I said, you may now append, dear Glaucon, * to the previous argument; the prison-house is the world of sight, the light of the fire is the sun, and you will not misapprehend me if you interpret the journey upwards to be the ascent of the soul into the intellectual world according to my poor belief, which, at your desire, I have expressed—whether rightly or wrongly God knows. But, whether true or false, my opinion is that in the world of knowledge the idea of good appears last of all, and is seen only with an effort; and, when seen, is also inferred to be the universal author of all things beautiful and right, parent of light and of the lord of light in this visible world. And the immediate source of reason and truth in the intellectual; and that this is the power upon which he who would act rationally either in public or private life must have his eye fixed. I agree, he said, as far as I am able to understand you.

Moreover, I said, you must not wonder that those who attain to this beatific vision are unwilling to descent to human affairs; for their souls are even hastening into the upper world where they desire to dwell; which desire of theirs is very natural, if our allegory may be trusted. Yes, very natural.

And is there anything surprising in one who passes from divine contemplations to the evil state of man, misbehaving himself in a ridiculous manner; if, while his eyes are blinking and before he has become accustomed to the surrounding darkness, he is compelled to fight in courts of law, or in other places, about the images or the shadows of images of justice, and is endeavoring to meet the conceptions of those who have never yet seen absolute justice? Anything but surprising, he replied.

Anyone who has common sense will remember that the bewilderments of the eyes are of two kinds, and arise from two causes, either from coming out of the light or from going into the light, which is true of the mind's eye, quite as much as of the bodily eye; and he who remembers this when he sees anyone whose vision is perplexed and weak, will not be too ready to laugh; he will first ask whether that soul of man has come out of the brighter life, and is unable to see because unaccustomed to the dark, or having turned from darkness to the day is dazzled by excess light. And he will count the one happy in his condition and state of being, and he will pity the others; or, if he have a mind to laugh at the soul which comes from below into the light, there will be more reason in this than in the laugh which greets him who returns from above to of the light into the den. That, he said, is a very just distinction.

But then, if I am right, certain professors of education must be wrong when they say that they can put knowledge into the soul which was not there before. Like sight into blind eyes. They undoubtedly say this, he replied. Whereas, our argument shows that the power of capacity of learning exists in the soul already; and that just as the eye was unable to turn from darkness to light without the whole body, so too the instruments of knowledge can only by the movement of the whole soul be turned from the world of becoming into that of being, and learn by degrees to endure the sight of being, and of the brightness of best of being, or in other words, of the good.

* Glaucon: one of the participants in the dialogue with Plato

©2010, 2017. Wheaton Press™ All Rights Reserved.

Coming Out of the Cave

- "You are my lamp, O Lord; the Lord turns my darkness into light." (2 Samuel 22:29)

- "He reveals the deep things of darkness and brings deep shadows into the light." (Job 12:22)

- "They grope in darkness with no light; he makes them stagger like drunkards." (Job 12:25)

- "When his lamp shone upon my head and by his light I walked through darkness!" (Job 29:3)

- "You, O Lord, keep my lamp burning; my God turns my darkness into light." (Psalm 18:28)

- "If I say, 'Surely the darkness will hide me and the light become night around me,' even the darkness will not be dark to you; the night will shine like the day, for darkness is as light to you." (Psalm 139:11-12)

- "Woe to those who call evil good and good evil, who put darkness for light and light for darkness, who put bitter for sweet and sweet for bitter." (Isaiah 5:20)

- "The people walking in darkness have seen a great light; on those living in the land of the shadow of death a light has dawned." (Isaiah 9:2)

- "So justice is far from us, and righteousness does not reach us. We look for light, but all is darkness; for brightness, but we walk in deep shadows." (Isaiah 59:9)

- "But if your eyes are bad, your whole body will be full of darkness. If then the light within you is darkness, how great is that darkness!" (Matthew 6:23)

- "This is the verdict: light has come into the world, but men loved darkness instead of light because their deeds were evil." (John 3:19)

- "Do everything without complaining or arguing, so that you may become blameless and pure, children of God without fault in a crooked and depraved generation, in which you shine like stars in the universe as you hold out the word of life." (Philippians 2:14-16)

- "For God, who said, 'Let light shine out of darkness', made his light shine in our hearts to give us the light of the knowledge of the glory of God in the face of Christ. (2 Corinthians 4:6)

- "When Jesus spoke again to the people, he said, 'I am the light of the world. Whoever follows me will never walk in darkness, but will have the light of life.'" (John 8:12)

 ©2010, 2017. Wheaton Press™ All Rights Reserved.

John 1 & The Cave:

Highlight all the connections you can find between The Cave and John Ch. 1.
Be prepared for discussion and sharing

1 In the beginning was the Word, and the Word was with God, and the Word was God.

2 He was with God in the beginning.

3 Through him all things were made; without him nothing was made that has been made.

4 In him was life, and that life was the light of all mankind.

5 The light shines in the darkness, and the darkness has not overcome it.

6 There was a man sent from God whose name was John.

7 He came as a witness to testify concerning that light, so that through him all might believe.

8 He himself was not the light; he came only as a witness to the light.

9 The true light that gives light to everyone was coming into the world.

10 He was in the world, and though the world was made through him, the world did not recognize him.

11 He came to that which was his own, but his own did not receive him.

12 Yet to all who did receive him, to those who believed in his name, he gave the right to become children of God —

13 children born not of natural descent, nor of human decision or a husband's will, but born of God.

14 The Word became flesh and made his dwelling among us. We have seen his glory, the glory of the one and only Son, who came from the Father, full of grace and truth.

15 (John testified concerning him. He cried out, saying, "This is the one I spoke about when I said, 'He who comes after me has surpassed me because he was before me.'")

16 Out of his fullness we have all received grace in place of grace already given.

17 For the law was given through Moses; grace and truth came through Jesus Christ.

18 No one has ever seen God, but the one and only Son, who is himself God and is in closest relationship with the Father, has made him known.

John 1:1-18

©2010, 2017. Wheaton Press™ All Rights Reserved.

Ephesians, Faith Island, the Trust List, and the Cave

Analyzing the Text

As you read this letter, pretend you are a member of the church at Ephesus and ask questions such as:

"Where are there connections to our discussions on belief, trust, faith, Faith Island, the Trust List, Plato's allegory of the cave, and the neo-Platonic look at Plato's work?"

In the space below write down at least three verses or passages in Ephesians that you find engaging, and briefly explain why you picked those verses.

 ©2010, 2017. Wheaton Press™ All Rights Reserved.

"Prophet Of MIRTH" Quotes & Notes; Doodles & Discussion:

Philip Yancey's article introducing us to the character and writing style of G.K. Chesterton.

KEY DISCUSSION TOPICS:

- Problem of Pleasure:

- All sin is warped good:

- "I'm Not Dead Yet!"

- More Class Notes:

©2010, 2017. Wheaton Press™ All Rights Reserved.

"How to Read CHESTERTON" Three Helpful Metaphors/Tips:

When I originally proposed this class to our board of trustees, Chesterton was shot down because his writing is difficult to comprehend. While reading Orthodoxy for the first time, you will not understand the value of certain passages or wording. When the same words are read years later, the earlier exposure helps build deeper meaning and understanding.

Metaphors may help us understand his writing a bit better. Western culture trains you to think, read and write linearly—like a train. The engine is a thesis statement, all the boxcars are evidence that support the thesis and the caboose is the conclusion. This sort of writing makes sense to most westerners. Here are some metaphors to explain how Chesterton writes:

Artwork public domain

Constellational Writing
Chesterton will make a cool point over here, look at this over there, and there is another idea. His unfolding various ideas are seemingly unconnected yet if you allow him to lead you through the chapter he ends by helping you step back and see a constellation. Look for the dots, note them as you read, leave them be, and at the end, you will say, "Oh! It is Orion!" Keep in mind that if you try to piece it together on your own, you might naturally be left confused. If you try to force the reading, I can almost guarantee you that it will be very confusing. Just read Chesterton, and then at the end of the chapter you will be given the bigger picture.

Making a Stew
In a seven course meal you make and serve each piece separately; you don't mix them all together. With stew, you take all the ingredients and throw it in a big pot. You stir it up, warm it and maybe even let it sit for some time. Then at the end it tastes delicious all mixed together. If you read Chesterton and try to digest it as you go (figure it out linearly), it would be like shoving celery salt, then raw meat, then carrots into your mouth; it will be confusing and might not taste good. Relax a bit and stop trying to figure it out linearly. Add the ingredients as you go into the crockpot of your mind and let the concepts simmer.... maybe even let is sit and cook for a few hours. Then take a taste.

Artwork public domain

Panning for GOLD!
If I were a student in my own class, I would want to think of this reading as panning for gold. Start scooping through the book, and keep going until something sticks out like gold in your pan. You may or may not have trouble reading this book; many of you may totally enjoy this book and may want to dig into it deeply. Either way, you don't need to understand all of it, but what you do understand will be worth it. I can almost guarantee you that you will find some gold nuggets of truth that can and will last a lifetime! Words are powerful. Truth is powerful. Take the time to look for some powerful witty words of truth in Chesterton.

Artwork public domain

 ©2010, 2017. Wheaton Press™ All Rights Reserved.

CHESTERTON Ch. 3 Orthodoxy "Suicide of Thought": Quotes to ponder and discuss

"Suicide of Thought" key questions & key notes (Lecture Notes from Mr. D.)

Chesterton ORTHODOX Ch3 "Suicide of Thought" Notes:

"It is idle to talk always of the alternative of reason and faith. Reason is itself a matter of faith. It is an act of faith to assert that our thoughts have any relation to reality at all."

"The young skeptic says, "I have a right to think for myself." But the old skeptic, the complete skeptic, says, "I have no right to think for myself. I have no right to think at all."

"There is a thought that stops thought. That is the only thought that ought to be stopped. That is the ultimate evil against which all religious authority was aimed. P 31:

"If the standard changes, how can there be improvement, which implies a standard?" P 33:

"Free thought has exhausted its own freedom This is an attack not upon the faith, but upon the mind; you cannot think if there are no things to think about. You cannot think if you are not separate from the subject of thought. Descartes said, "I think; therefore I am." The philosophic evolutionist reverses and negatives the epigram. He says, "I am not; therefore I cannot think."

"To sum up our contention so far, we may say that the most characteristic current philosophies have not only a touch of mania, but a touch of suicidal mania. The mere questioner has knocked his head against the limits of human thought; and cracked it. You cannot fancy a more skeptical world than that in which men doubt if there is a world."

"We have no more questions left to ask. We have looked for questions in the darkest corners and on the wildest peaks. We have found all the questions that can be found. It is time we gave up looking for questions and began looking for answers." P.34

"Every act of will is an act of self-limitation. To desire action is to desire limitation. In that sense every act is an act of self-sacrifice. When you choose anything, you reject everything else. That objection, which men of this school used to make to the act of marriage, is really an objection to every act. Every act is an irrevocable selection exclusion. Just as when you marry one woman you give up all the others, so when you take one course of action you give up all the other courses. P.36

"By rebelling against everything he has lost his right to rebel against anything. P. 38

"But, indeed, Nietzsche will stand very well as the type of the whole of this failure of abstract violence. The softening of the brain which ultimately overtook him was not a physical accident. If Nietzsche had not ended in imbecility, Nietzscheism would end in imbecility. Thinking in isolation and with pride ends in being an idiot. Every man who will not have softening of the heart must at last have softening of the brain." P.39

"So he who wills to reject nothing, wills the destruction of will; for will is not only the choice of something, but the rejection of almost everything."

"There is a giant of whom we see only the lopped arms and legs walking about." p.41

"They have torn the soul of Christ into silly strips, labeled egoism and altruism, and they are equally puzzled by His insane magnificence and His insane meekness. They have parted His garments among them, and for His vesture they have cast lots; though the coat was without seam woven from the top throughout." P.41

©2010, 2017. Wheaton Press™ All Rights Reserved.

CHESTERTON Ch. 3 Orthodoxy "Suicide of Thought": Choice and Free Will

"Suicide of Thought" key questions & key notes
Answer these questions with a partner before discussion.

"There is a thought that stops all thought, and that is the only thought that aught to be stopped." P. 31

1. What is it?

2. How do I get in?

3. How do I get out?

 ©2010, 2017. Wheaton Press™ All Rights Reserved.

How and What to Trust

It is essential to understand that there are two functional and accepted types of truths. Speaker and teacher Mike Penninga[1] states that various truths can end up in two different "Truth Buckets": Subjective and Objective.

Many people who approach philosophy and theology confuse this issue. Worse yet, many people have built a lifestyle from various philosophies and theologies, especially concerning morality, with a deep misunderstanding of this foundational approach to reality.

When building a house to live in it is important to use the right materials at the right time in the right way. With weak axioms, we end up with a cracked, crumbling, leaky basement. When we confuse objective and subjective truths, it is like mixing mortar that is unsuitable for building a wall out of. It will look solid, but it will be weak and unsafe. When we lean on the wall or put any pressure on the wall, it will most likely come crashing down with devastating effect. Often the person who has made this mistake is blind or ignorant to this misappropriation of truth and what they are trusting, so they feel awkward at best and utterly foolish or defeated at worst when light is shed on the mistake.

In light of some of these issues, devastating personal and communal consequences can result from a simple lack of awareness or from intentional ignorance and denial about the healthy practice of appropriate differentiation of the buckets into which we place truths. Furthermore, this responsibility has exponential impact on leaders! Teachers, parents, and mentors must clearly and continually articulate into which bucket they are putting the various lessons they teach.

Subjective truths are purely based on the perspective of the subject (person) making the decision; they are relative concepts based only on personal preference, opinion, and perspective. These truths tell us more about the subject (the person and his or her feelings or opinions) than the object (the issue or item) in question.

Some subjective truths are:
Vanilla ice cream is the best flavor.
Your stained glass window is beautiful and inspiring.
Ice cream is delicious.
It is a beautiful day outside.

Photo public domain

Objective truths are true regardless of the perspective or feelings of the person making the decision or observation; it is a universally trusted standard. These truths are focused entirely on the object in question rather than the subject (the person and his or her perspective, feelings, or opinions about the item or issue).

Some objective truths are:
Insulin lowers blood sugar levels and can help manage diabetes.
The stained glass window is broken.
There are a wide variety of ice cream flavors.
It is sunny and seventy degrees outside with a gentle breeze.

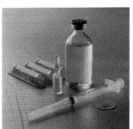
Photo public domain

An axiom is a premise ~~of~~ or starting point of reasoning

classically defined an axiom is a premise so ccdec as to

©2010, 2017. Wheaton Press™ All Rights Reserved.

PERSPECTIVES ON PERFECTION AND MORALITY

We need to become familiar with the tools for building our worldview home and personal trust list on our search for Truth. Later we will see that there are real choices to be made with real differences and profound, life-affecting consequences connected to those choices. Hopefully this is all becoming clearer as we finish setting the stage (Faith Island), continue to get to know the four main characters (the trust lists), develop the plot (our collective search for Truth and a clear picture of Prime Reality), and start unearthing the sub-plot (developing your own firm and functional personal trust list).

Four Perspectives on Morality

Morality is a challenging word to explain because of the types, layers, implications, and functions of morality. Your attitude and perspective toward morality directly relate to how you define these terms and how you choose to interpret subjectivity versus objectivity. That choice in turn directly influences your daily behavior and decision making. What we are most concerned with is where the authority and standards come from for these decisions. Do we simply get to decide what to do with our time and money and bodies? Does someone else decide? Or does an objective, absolute standard exist for everybody to follow?

Idealism:

For a pure idealist, morality is objective based on the nature of the spiritual Ideal as eternally good, beautiful, and true. Moral behavior and decisions are defined as right and good based on the perfect ideal of what is good, beautiful, and true However, morality feels subjective for idealists living on Faith Island based on each person's imperfect and incomplete personal interpretation of and limited access to the spiritually ideal, objective standards of what is perfectly good, perfectly beautiful, and perfectly true. It is intrinsically difficult for that which is imperfect and, broken, unformed, and ugly to know and understand, let alone do and be, perfectly good, beautiful and true.

Materialism:

For an authentic materialist, morality is subjective at the core. It is internal and relative based completely on perspective and preference, like choosing an ice cream flavor. Because there is nothing objective outside of and distinct from the cause and effect nature of the material realm, morality appears to be based on self (on individual humans) with no actual, real, objective authority or standards. However, morality feels objective when powerful people or organizations enforce individual or group preferences, or when a community gives authority to a majority or a select group of people. This feeling of objectivity can be subtly misleading for many materialists. Such moral standards are not actually objective; rather, they are the result of subjective majority preference.

Monism:

For a complete monist, morality is wholly subjective and is basically the same as that of a materialist. The difference is that the weight of one's preference often carries greater authority, because a monist can claim to be part of the universal being often called "god." In short, good and evil, right and wrong behavior and standards are based on the understanding of self as being part of the collective universe which exists as god. The self is part of the universal, absolute authority of humanity's collective coexistence. However, morality for a monist, like that of a materialist feels objective when moral "preference" is universally established, usually through human loyalty or majority rule. Moral standards can be objectified by tradition and rituals or by allegiance to a preferred aspect of behavior or a preferred standard. This often ends up manifesting itself in the form of allegiance to a "side" drawn from the dualistic and polarized nature of reality on planet Earth, such as light and dark, birth and death, creation and decay, etc...

Theism:

For a sincere theist, ethical morality for humans is objective based on the nature of the Creator God as the definer of and standard for Morality. However, because God is a perfect, autonomous Being separate from creation and from created beings, morality is actually subjective for God who has the intrinsic power and authority to define morality. However, because perfection is that which cannot be improved upon and that which has no flaw, even though God is a living Being, God will never change moral standards. Interestingly for theists, morality often feels subjective in a similar way that perfection can feel subjective since it is based on one's personal interpretation of and limited access to God, God's nature, God's Word, and God's revelation. This is where different religions and denominations within these religions can have a wide variety of moral standards, but all of them say they are based on God's perfect standards.

 ©2010, 2017. Wheaton Press™ All Rights Reserved.

PERSPECTIVES ON PERFECTION AND MORALITY

Four Perspectives on Perfection

Your attitude and perspective toward perfection directly relate to how you behave and make decisions all the time. Is perfection subjective or objective? After death are we able to become one with perfection or dwell with a perfect God?

Idealism:

For pure idealists, perfection and wholeness comprise a objective ideal state of being, based on the nature of the "Spiritual Ideal." This is because idealists trust that only the ideal spiritual realm is really real. For idealists, the material world is broken; it is not ideal and can always be improved upon. If we want to exist forever, we must strive until we actually become that one, perfect ideal that is spiritual, not physical. Perfection is that which is eternally good, beautiful, and true. There is only one "form" of perfection. It is eternal because it is perfect and will last forever in that state. It has no flaw; it is the only standard by which all things are measured. For idealists, perfection is objective; It exists as true and perfect whether humans like it or know it.

Imagine the ideal car. It never runs out of gas, never breaks down, and never rusts. That car does not exist on Earth yet. But, the idea of a car will last longer than any physical car will. If all the cars on the planet vanished, the idea of that car would still remain! We could almost call this trust list "idea-ism." Every year I ask my students to close their eyes and imagine the perfect human being. They can all talk about a perfect human being, but nobody has met one. I ask them if any of them thought of themselves and in twenty years of teaching, nobody has ever had the image of their current self come to mind.

Materialism:

For an authentic materialist, perfection and wholeness are literally in the eye of the beholder, and therefore they are utterly and completely relative and subjective. Because there is no outside, objective standard for perfection, and because everybody has their own unique, individual, personal perspective on the world from within the world, materialists have no authoritative, purely objective standard for making verifiable comparisons. People can agree on standards, or they can pretend that there is objectivity, but this is fabricated and malleable.

Monism:

For an authentic monist perfection and wholeness are part of existence; therefore, everything is perfect as it exists. This is similar to the materialist perspective on perfection; it simply adds in the weight of spirituality. Monists will concede that there is nothing objective, above, beyond or separate from the universal collective coexistence of everything. Consequently, the concept of perfection is always subjective, because there is nothing that is distinct from the unified existence of the universe. As such, monists do not believe in an all-powerful creator God in the sense that theists do, so there is no basis for any objective comparison or standard. Often a monist will refer to existence with authoritative vocabulary like "god" or "the unifying life force." A monist believes everything in existence to be a part and parcel of god who in nature fits the definition of perfection as that which cannot be improved upon. Therefore, everything is perfect as it is, if only we had the eyes and willingness to see it as such. All of that which exists is perfect simply because it exists.

Theism:

Perfection and wholeness exist as defined by an objective, perfect, living Being. This Being is perfect, cannot be improved upon, eternal, and complete. This Being is also distinct and independent from creation and from created beings. In theism, this Being is usually referred to as God. God as the perfect creator has the objectivity and authority to decide or declare what is perfect. Thus, humanity is subject to God's definition of and standards for perfection. This is a great place to see an axiom come into play: Because God is perfect, God will have perfect standards; therefore, one would have to be perfect to dwell with this perfect Being. Another interesting point on perfection for theists surfaces when created human beings reject or differ on their interpretation of or relationship with God the perfect standard of perfection.

©2010, 2017. Wheaton Press™ All Rights Reserved.

PERSPECTIVES ON PERFECTION AND MORALITY

Reflections on Morality and Perfection

While there is some overlap between these different trust lists, there are also differences that are polar opposites. For example, theism is similar to idealism, but instead of a state of existence, or an abstract concept, "form," or idea, this Being is alive, interacts with creation and created beings, and has authority over these other beings. Thus, there is the potential for unlimited, independent definitions of perfection and wholeness as defined by this objective, perfect Authority. Theism is also different than monism: In theism God is separate from creation like an artist is separate from a painting. In monism, everything is god; the painting is god and god is the painting.

These definitions shape not only our perception and understanding of reality, but they also shape how we relate to each other on a daily basis. When we fail to understand that different people in a single conversation may be utilizing the same word to describe separate perspectives with vastly different consequences, we delve into a world of misunderstanding based on false assumption.

Imagine four people having a cup of coffee and discussing perfection. An authentic materialist and a complete monist would get along pretty well as they discuss the differences and similarities on what is perfect. There is no heaven or hell or objective standard, just undiluted freedom to describe perfection based off of whatever standard is preferential.

The pure idealist and the sincere theist could debate the standards and sources they trust to define what is perfect. A theist might discuss access to this standard through a personal relationship with this Living Being called God. An idealist will most likely describe this standard as a state of being. While a theist spends time with God in a relationship, this state of perfect existence that an idealist calls god is not a Being that an idealist could spend time with. An idealist strives to become one with this ideal one existence. An idealist would need to become god and become perfect in order to exist as god. For the theist, because this perfect God has perfect standards, the theist would need to become perfect according to God's standards in order to dwell with this God. However, a theist never becomes God. This conversations between a theist and an idealist would naturally turn into a discussion on the methodology for attaining and sustaining this state of perfection.

Philosophy does not necessarily show us what the religions believe and practice; it shows us why religions do what they do and offer what they offer. When we layer the objective and subjective concepts with ideas like perfection and morality, the contrasts and the chasms start to get much wider and deeper.

PLEASE REMEMBER:

We all are trying to figure out this stuff as best we can using what we deem as trustworthy. Learning about the critical differences between these four worldview perspectives should help us humbly approach conversations with a listening ear and an open heart. It is of vital importance to firmly plant a stake in what you trust to be true. Paradoxically, it is also of vital importance to know that what you believe to be true is believed or trusted; not "proved" or "100% objectively verified."

   ©2010, 2017. Wheaton Press™ All Rights Reserved.

What and How to Trust

Notes and personal connections to the subjective—objective map

Work in a small group to create two examples of **subjective** truths

For you personally:
1)

2)

For your family:
1)

2)

For your school:
1)

2)

For your culture:
1)

2)

Work in a small group to create two examples of **objective** truths

For you personally:
1)

2)

For your family:
1)

2)

For your school:
1)

2)

For your culture:
1)

2)

What and How to Trust

Create 5 distinct questions about subjective and objective truth. Use these questions to interview someone who is not in this class, and write down his or her responses. Come to class prepared to share in our class discussion.

Question #1: _____

Response #1:

Question #2: _____

Response #2:

Question #3: _____

Response #3:

Question #4: _____

Response #4

Question #5: _____

Response #5:

Below, write a short personal response to our discussion on subjective and objective truth. List at least three new insights you have about this topic that is essential to philosophy and theology.

 ©2010, 2017. Wheaton Press™ All Rights Reserved.

Unit 2
(ACT 2)

Philosophy
and the
4 Trust Lists

Philosophy & Theology
INVITED TO TRUST

UNIT 2 (Act 2) ESSENTIAL QUESTIONS:

1. What are the four major World Views and their different Trust Lists
2. What are key consequences of trusting varying answers to the seven core questions of philosophy?
3. What does a Pure Idealist trust?
4. What does an Authentic Materialist trust?
5. What does a Complete Monist trust?
6. What does a Religious Theist trust?

UNIT 2 (Act 2) READINGS:

1. Dominguez, Matthew "Trust"
2. "Words of the Buddha"
3. *Philippians*
4. Nietzsche, Friedrich "The Madman"
5. Keats, John "When I Have Fears That I May Cease To Be"
6. *Ecclesiastes*
7. Weir, Andy "The Egg"
8. *I John*
9. Jennings, Mason "I Love You and Buddha Too"
10. *John*

UNIT 2 (Act 2) THINKBOOK LEARNING OPPORTUNITIES:

Formative:

- ❏ Philosophy Trust Lists Pre-Assessment Quiz
- ❏ Scripture Reading "Truth Revealed": Philippians (Idealism)
- ❏ Scripture Reading "Truth Revealed": Ecclesiastes (Materialism)
- ❏ Scripture Reading "Truth Revealed": I John (Monism)
- ❏ Scripture Reading "Truth Revealed": John (Religious Theism)

UNIT 2 (Act 2) LEARNING PLAN:

1. An Introduction to the World of Philosophy and the Four World Views
2. Pure Idealism
3. Authentic Materialism
4. Complete Monism
5. Religious Theism

 ©2010, 2017. Wheaton Press™ All Rights Reserved.

Notes "Philosophy as a POWERFUL tool":

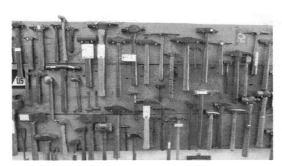

Artwork public domain

"With Great Power there must also come great responsibility" (Uncle Ben in Spiderman)

THE NEED TO LOVE!

Revisit 1 Corinthians 13: Discussion Notes.

Love Is the Greatest

13 If I could speak all the languages of earth and of angels, but didn't love others, I would only be a noisy gong or a clanging cymbal. 2 If I had the gift of prophecy, and if I understood all of God's secret plans and possessed all knowledge, and if I had such faith that I could move mountains, but didn't love others, I would be nothing. 3 If I gave everything I have to the poor and even sacrificed my body, I could boast about it;[a] but if I didn't love others, I would have gained nothing.

4 Love is patient and kind. Love is not jealous or boastful or proud 5 or rude. It does not demand its own way. It is not irritable, and it keeps no record of being wronged. 6 It does not rejoice about injustice but rejoices whenever the truth wins out. 7 Love never gives up, never loses faith, is always hopeful, and endures through every circumstance.

8 Prophecy and speaking in unknown languages[b] and special knowledge will become useless. But love will last forever! 9 Now our knowledge is partial and incomplete, and even the gift of prophecy reveals only part of the whole picture! 10 But when the time of perfection comes, these partial things will become useless.

11 When I was a child, I spoke and thought and reasoned as a child. But when I grew up, I put away childish things. 12 Now we see things imperfectly, like puzzling reflections in a mirror, but then we will see everything with perfect clarity.[c] All that I know now is partial and incomplete, but then I will know everything completely, just as God now knows me completely.

13 Three things will last forever—faith, hope, and love—and the greatest of these is love.

1 Corinthians 13 New Living Translation (NLT)

©2010, 2017. Wheaton Press™ All Rights Reserved.

The Trust Lists on one page:

Views of Reality & Core Philosophy Questions	IDEALISM (Platonism)	MATERIALISM (Atheism)	Monism (Pantheism)	RELIGIOUS THEISM (Monotheism)
1. What is the Nature of Reality? What is really real? Two options: Material & Spiritual	A Pure Idealist trusts **that ONLY the Spiritual is really real** and that Reality is a state of eternal spiritual perfection.	An Authentic Materialist trusts **that ONLY the Material (the Natural) is really real**; there is no spiritual realm.	A Complete Monist trusts **that the Spiritual and the Material are BOTH really real, existing as one entity.** Reality presents itself as dual in nature yet All of existence is ultimately ONE universal interconnected unity.	A Religious Theist trusts **that the Spiritual and the Material are BOTH real yet independent, interdependent, and intradependent with each other.**
2. Who/what is God?	A Pure Idealist trusts that the impersonal eternal perfect Spiritual Ideal is what people often call "god"; it is absolute complete Truth, Beauty, and, Goodness.	An Authentic Materialist trusts that There is no objective powerful being outside of the material. God is a figment of man's creativity and imagination, a creative idea or concept.	A Complete Monist trusts that everything is "god" – that everything and everybody in the universe is an integral interconnected part of the unity of life called "god."	A Religious Theist trusts that there is a distinct God that is the all-powerful Creator, the sustainer, and the giver of all of life. God is personal and has personality.
3. Who is Man? What is Mankind? What is a human being? *(Who am I? What am I?)*	A Pure Idealist trusts that humans exist as one of the infinite incomplete imperfect replicas or "shadows" of the real (eternal) Ideal state of spiritual perfection.	An Authentic Materialist trusts that human beings are a fascinating, unique, and highly complex system of matter and electricity that is beautifully aware of "self" and "others."	A Complete Monist trusts that a human is a unique unrepeatable part and parcel of "god"; we are part of the one body of the universe and the entirety of reality referred to as "god."	A Religious Theist trusts that humans are a distinct wonderful creation made in the image of God but not possessing the exact nature of God nor existing as an extension or part of God.
4. What is the basis of and standard for morality: Right and Wrong, and Authority?	A Pure Idealist trusts that all morality is **objective** and based on the nature of the impersonal perfect "Ideal One" the Spiritual Ideal, which is Absolute Truth, Perfect Beauty, and Complete Goodness.	An Authentic Materialist trusts that all morality is ultimately **subjective** and based exclusively or collectively on self, majority, and power.	A Complete Monist trusts that morality is completely **subjective** based 'souly' on one's individual preference as a part of the interconnected universal reality called "god" and thus morality is relative in nature.	A Religious Theist trusts that all Ethical morality is **objective** based on the personal all-powerful nature of God who is Perfect and Good. God (and God's word and nature) is the standard for and author of morality.
5. What happens to a human at death?	A Pure Idealist trusts that when we die perfection is attained and we become one with the state of spiritual perfection; and (or) we cease to exist as image of perfection and as an imperfect "self".	An Authentic Materialist trusts that humans cease to be "aware" of one's existence at the point of death.	A Complete Monist trusts that when a human "dies" we literally "morph" into another part of existence and another component of the universal reality, which is "god."	A Religious Theist trusts that when humans die we obtain individual perfection and exist eternally in continual relationship with the perfect personal God OR we remain in an imperfect incomplete state and necessarily exist separated from God.
6. What is the meaning and purpose of human history? What is the essence of human interaction and relationships?	A Pure Idealist trusts that history and human memory are records of humans striving to escape nonexistence and attain an ideal state of spiritual perfection.	An Authentic Materialist trusts that History is a story of a linear sequence of events and phenomena linked by cause and effect in a closed system (such as natural selection). Human interaction is literally chemistry and pure cause and effect.	A Complete Monist trusts that history and human memory consist of the repository of collective memories of our collective coexistence as "god."	A Religious Theist trusts that history is a "linear, meaningful sequence of events leading to the fulfillment of God's purposes for man" in an open system (James Sire, *Universe Next Door*). History is THE True Epic Adventure Story of God's interaction with mankind.
7. Why are we here? Where are we going? What is the purpose of Human existence? *(To be or not to be? What is the purpose of living for tomorrow?)*	A Pure Idealist trusts that we exist only to achieve and sustain an ideal state of spiritual perfection.	An Authentic Materialist trusts that humans get to create their own individual and collective meaning for life.	A Complete Monist trusts that every human has the exciting opportunity to continue experiencing being various components of universal reality—of "god" – forever.	A Religious Theist trusts that at least one reason that humans exist is to enjoy and experience a meaningful relationship with the Creator and Sustainer of Life.

William E Brown

You may not live what you profess; but you live what you believe, what you trust. It is inescapable!

 ©2010, 2017. Wheaton Press™ All Rights Reserved.

A Closer Look at Pure Idealism

We use what we trust to formulate our conclusions concerning the nature of reality.

PURE IDEALISM (Platonism):   We are striving to exist as Spiritual Perfection, the Spiritual Ideal.
(as "God" or as part of "God")

Artwork public domain

Pure Idealists trust that only the Spiritual is the eternal fabric of Prime Reality. True Idealists, Idea-ists, have a foundational understanding that the non-material "Perfected Idea" has an eternal, beautiful, true, and good weight and real-ness to it that supersedes any physical attempt to replicate and materialize this "True Idea." This understanding leads them to a greater awareness that this weight or realness of the ideal is manifested in a spiritual reality and is merely, often poorly, represented (re-presented) in the physical. For all of the physical world, but particularly for humans, this situation is exactly accurate; humans are essentially "imperfect shadows" or "incomplete imitations" of the Ideal Spiritual and are literally trying to become "One with Ultimate Reality" which is an enlightened state of Spiritual Perfection. Currently, humans are imperfect and exist on earth only as the unlimited various representations of imperfect "images" of perfection and as potential for actual eternal existence in a state of perfection in the real Ideal Perfect Spiritual Realm. Humans are personally responsible for making themselves into the Ideal, for becoming perfectly good, beautiful, and true in order to exist fully and eternally as Spiritual Perfection and to actualize eternally escaping nonexistence as an incomplete shadowy replica.

"THE ONE"

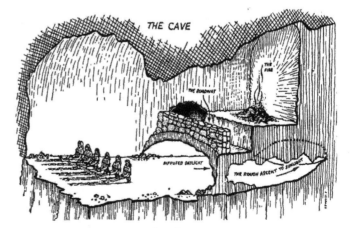

THE CAVE

"THE ESCELATION OF THE SOUL"

Absolute Any being arises or ideas that exists whether or not
Any mind posies, or existwe or reflexts its attibutes

©2010, 2017. Wheaton Press™ All Rights Reserved.

PURE IDEALISM: Reality Check, Research, Religions, Relevancy, Recognition...

Cultural Connections:

Poetry and Books:

Film:

Music:

Religion:

Sacred Texts:

Historical Figures:

Influential/Famous People:

Key Landmarks/Historical Significance:

 ©2010, 2017. Wheaton Press™ All Rights Reserved.

Learning Assessment
Words of the Buddha

1. Read and ponder some of the common words of the Buddha.

1. Write a general response to the popular Buddhist truths, quotes, and parables you encountered.

2. Locate and write out Bible verses and their references next to the Buddhist quotes that support, are similar to, or are antithetical to these words of the Buddha. What did you observe during this exercise?

1. Which of these would you tweet or post on social media? Why? Which ones would you not tweet or post on your social media?

1. What are 3 or 4 new insights about idealism do you have after this exercise?

Common "Words of the Buddha"

1. **The First Noble Truth**—the nature of suffering (Dukkha): This is the noble truth of suffering. Birth is suffering, aging is suffering, illness is suffering, death is suffering; sorrow, lamentation, pain, grief, and despair are suffering; union with what is displeasing is suffering; separation from what is pleasing is suffering; not to get what one wants is suffering; in brief, the five aggregates subject to clinging are suffering.

2. **The Second Noble Truth**—suffering's origin (Dukkha Samudaya): This is the noble truth of the origin of suffering. It is this craving that leads to renewed existence, accompanied by delight and lust, seeking delight here and there, that is, craving for sensual pleasures, craving for existence, craving for extermination.

3. **The Third Noble Truth**—suffering's cessation (Dukkha Nirodha): This is the noble truth of the cessation of suffering: it is the remainder less fading away and cessation of that same craving, the giving up and relinquishing of it, freedom from it, non-reliance on it.

4. **The Fourth Noble Truth**—the path (Dukkha Nirodha Gamini Patipada Magga) leading to the cessation of suffering: this is the noble truth of the way leading to the cessation of suffering: it is the Noble Eightfold Path; that is, right view, right intention, right speech, right action, right livelihood, right effort, right mindfulness, right concentration.

5. Be a lamp unto yourself. Work out your liberation with diligence.

6. Desire is the root cause of all miseries.

7. Do not think lightly of evil that not the least consequence will come of it. A whole water pot will fill up from dripping drops of water. A fool himself with evil, just a little at a time.

8. Ennui *(boredom)* has made more gamblers than avarice, more drunkards than thirst, and perhaps as many suicides as despair.

9. For all mortals, birth is suffering, aging is suffering, and sickness is suffering.

10. Hatred does not cease by hatred, but only by love. This is the eternal rule.

11. He is able who thinks he is able.

12. Life is suffering.

13. I reached in experience the nirvana that is unborn, unrivalled, secure from attachment, un-decaying and unstained. This condition is indeed reached by me that is deep, difficult to see, difficult to understand, tranquil, excellent, beyond the reach of mere logic, subtle, and to be realized only by the wise. I've got children. I've got wealth. This is the way a fool brings suffering on himself. He does not even own himself, so how can he have children or wealth?

14. A family is a place where minds come in contact with one another. If these minds love one another the home will be as beautiful as a flower garden. But if these minds get out of harmony with one another it is like a storm that plays havoc with the garden.

15. A good friend who points out mistakes and imperfections and rebukes evil is to be respected as if he reveals a secret hidden treasure.

16. A wise man, recognizing that the world is but an illusion, does not act as if it is real, so he escapes the suffering.

17. If a man possesses a repentant spirit his sins will disappear, but if he has an unrepentant spirit his sins will continue and condemn him for their sake forever.

 ©2010, 2017. Wheaton Press™ All Rights Reserved.

Common "Words of the Buddha"

18. If a man's mind becomes pure, his surroundings will also become pure.

19. A visiting Zen student asked Ajahn Chah, "How old are you? Do you live here all year round?" "I live nowhere", he replied. "There is no place you can find me. I have no age. To have age, you must exist, and to think you exist is already a problem. Don't make problems., then the world has none either. Don't make a self. There's nothing more to say." (Ajahn Chah)

20. A woman wanted to know how to deal with anger. I asked when anger arose whose anger it was. She said it was hers. Well, if it really was her anger, then she should be able to tell it to go away, shouldn't she? But it really isn't hers to command. Holding on to anger as a personal possession will cause suffering. If anger really belonged to us, it would have to obey us. If it doesn't obey us, that means it's only a deception. Don't' fall for it. Whenever the mind is happy or sad, don't fall for it. It's all a deception. (Ajahn Chah)

21. He who loves 50 people has 50 woes. He who loves no one has no woes.

22. An insincere and evil friend is more to be feared than a wild beast. A wild beast may wound your body, but an evil friend will wound your mind.

23. Believe nothing, no matter where you read it, or who said it, no matter if I have said it, unless it agrees with your reason and your own common sense.

24. Do not accept any of my words on faith, believing them just because I said them. Be like an analyst buying gold, who cuts, burns, and critically examines his product for authenticity. Only accept what passes the test by proving useful and beneficial in your life.

25. Do not believe what your teacher tells you merely out of respect for the teacher.

26. Do not dwell in the past, do not dream of the future, concentrate the mind on the present moment.

27. Do not examine the limitations of others. Examine how you can change your own.

28. Do not overrate what you received, nor envy others. He who envies others does not obtain peace of mind.

29. Embrace nothing. If you meet the Buddha, kill the Buddha. If you meet your father, kill your father. Only live your life as it is, not bound to anything. ("kill the Buddha" is like Jesus saying "hate your mother and father" – The One is not the Buddha & the Buddha is not the One!)

30. Endurance is one of the most difficult disciplines, but it is to the one who endures that the final victory comes.

31. Even death is not to be feared by one who has lived wisely.

32. Every human being is the author of his own health or disease.

33. It is wrong to think that misfortunes come from the east or from the west. They originate within one's own mind. Therefore, it is foolish to guard against misfortunes from the external world and leave the inner mind uncontrolled.

34. Holding on to anger is like grasping a hot coal with the intent of throwing it at someone else. You are the one who gets burned.

35. However many holy words you read, however many you speak, what good will they do to you if you do not act upon them?

©2010, 2017. Wheaton Press™ All Rights Reserved.

Common "Words of the Buddha"

36. Let us rise up and be thankful, for if we didn't learn a lot today, at least we learned a little, and if we didn't learn a little, at least we didn't get sick, and if we got sick, at least we didn't die; so, let us all be thankful.

37. From what is dear, grief is born, from what is dear, fear is born. For someone freed from what is dear there is no grief—so why fear?
From what is loved, grief is born, from what is loved, fear is born. For someone freed from what is loved, there is no grief—so why fear?
From delight, grief is born, from delight, fear is born. For someone freed from delight there is no grief—so why fear?
From sensuality, grief is born, from sensuality, fear is born. For someone freed from sensuality there is no grief—so why fear?
From craving, grief is born, from craving, fear is born. For someone freed from craving there is no grief—so why fear?

38. It is a man's own mind, not his enemy or foe, that lures him to evil ways.

39.. Just as a candle cannot burn without fire, men cannot live without a spiritual life.

40. Let a man avoid evil deeds as a man who loves life avoids poison.

41.. My doctrine is not a doctrine but just a vision. I have not given you any set rules. I have not given you a system.

42. Our life is the creation of our mind.

43. Peace comes from within. Do not seek it from without.

44.. The Buddha does but tells the way. It is for you to swelter at the task.

45. The thought manifests as the word; the word manifests as the deed; the deed develops into habit; and habit hardens into character. So watch the thought and its ways with care, and let it spring from love born out of concern for all beings.

46.. The tongue is like a sharp knife. It kills without drawing blood.

47. There are only two mistakes one can make along the road to truth: not going all the way, and not starting.

48.. There has to be evil so that good can prove its purity above it.

49.. No one saves us but ourselves. No one can and no one may. We ourselves must walk the path.

50. Learn to let go. That is the key to happiness.

51. There is only one time when it is essential to awaken. That time is now.

52. Therefore, be ye lamps unto yourselves, be a refuge to yourselves. Hold fast to truth as a lamp; hold fast to the truth as a refuge. Look not for a refuge in anyone beside yourselves. And those, who shall be a lamp unto themselves, shall betake themselves to no external refuge, but holding fast to the truth as their lamp, and holding fast to the truth as their refuge, they shall reach the topmost height.

53. This existence of ours is as transient as autumn clouds.

54.. Thousands of candles can be lighted from a single candle, and the life of the candle will not be shortened. Happiness never decreases by being shared.

 ©2010, 2017. Wheaton Press™ All Rights Reserved.

Common "Words of the Buddha"

55. To live a pure unselfish life, one must count nothing as one's own in the midst of abundance.

56. To understand everything is to forgive everything.

57. Unity can only be manifested by the binary. Unity itself and the idea of unity are already two.

58. Virtue is persecuted more by the wicked than it is loved by the good.

59. What we think, we become.

60. Words have the power to both destroy and heal. When words are both true and kind, they can change our world.

61. Work out your own salvation. Do not depend on others.

62. It is better to travel well than to arrive.

63. The trouble is that you think you have time.

64. The whole secret of existence is to have no fear.

65. You are all the Buddha.

67. You cannot travel the path until you have become the path itself.

68. You have to start giving first and expect absolutely nothing. You only lose what you cling to.

69. You will not be punished for your anger, you will be punished by your anger.

70. You, yourself, as much as anybody in the entire universe, deserve your love and affection.

71. If we could see the miracle of a single flower clearly, our whole life would change.

72. If we can know, there's no need to believe.

73. I am the miracle.

©2010, 2017. Wheaton Press™ All Rights Reserved.

Scripture Reading Integrity Assignments
Philippians and idealism

Read and annotate the letter to the church at Philippi from the Apostle Paul in one sitting. Pretend you are a member of that church. Where do you see connections to our discussion on idealism and the religions, ways, and "isms" that base their Trust List on this philosophical approach to reality? The connections you make can be subtle, overt, literary, historical, artistic, personal, or metaphoric. How does Philippians 3:8 speak to an idealist or a "Christian Idealist" in a unique and profound way.

In the space below, write down at least three verses that you find engaging, and briefly explain why you picked those verses. Cut and paste or write out the entire verse, but do not simply put the reference. Do not summarize the verse as a response.

2:13 For its God who works in you to will and to act in order to fulfill his good purpose

1:14 because of my chains most of the brothers and sisters have become confident of God and dare all the more to the proclaim the gospel without fear

4:8 Family brothers and sisters whatever is true whatever is noble whatever is right whatever is pure whatever is lovely whatever is admirable if anything is excellent or praiseworthy think about such things

Photo courtesy of Prince MRD

©2010, 2017. Wheaton Press™ All Rights Reserved.

A Closer look at Authentic Materialism

We use what we trust to formulate our conclusions concerning the nature of reality.

MATERIALISM (Atheism):   We are our own individual gods; there is no objective God to become, to serve, submit to, or to dwell with. We simply are.

Artwork public domain

Authentic Materialists trust that the composition of Prime Reality is only that which can be observed and measured materially. No Actual Real Spirituality or Spiritual realm exists. Humans are beautiful complex systems of matter and electricity who are subjected to an intricate arrangement of pure cause and effect and awesomely "aware" of their immediate unfolding presence in time and space. The impression of the Ideal or Perfect is a completely subjective, relative concept. Consistent Materialists believe that Humans can do and be whatever they prefer, so long as they avoid negative natural consequences while simultaneously and paradoxically acknowledging that this freedom is arbitrary and ultimately a façade; life is actually an unfolding passive adventure of random electronic reactionary impulses. Consistent and authentic Materialists unabashedly and wholeheartedly embrace that Life is ultimately absurd and beautifully or grotesquely ridiculous; therefore, genuine Materialists assert that humans can attempt to "create" their own sense of adventure, purpose, and meaning and live out their awareness in the most personally pleasurable ways available while seeking and hoping to achieve positive natural consequences and avoid negative natural consequences.

©2010, 2017. Wheaton Press™ All Rights Reserved.

AUTHENTIC MATERIALISM: Reality Check, Research, Religions, Relevancy, Recognition…

Cultural Connections:

Poetry and Books:

Film:

Music:

Religion:

Sacred Texts:

Historical Figures:

Influential/Famous People:

Key Landmarks/Historical Significance:

70   ©2010, 2017. Wheaton Press™ All Rights Reserved.

A Closer look at Authentic Materialism

When I Have Fear That I May Cease To Be

When I have fears that I may cease to be
Before my pen has glean'd my teeming brain,
Before high piled books, in charact'ry.
Hold like rich garners the full-ripen'd grain;
When I behold, upon the night's starr'd face,
Huge cloudy symbols of a high romance,
And think that I may never live to trace
Their shadows, with the magic hand of chance;
And when I fell, fair creature of an hour!
That I shall never look upon thee more,
Never have relish in the faery power
Of unreflecting love! — then on the shore
Of the wide world I stand alone, and think
Till love and fame to nothingness do sink.

Published in 1848; taken from Poets.org public domain http://www.poets.org/poetsorg/poem/when-i-have-fears-i-may-cease-to-be)

Author Bio: Born in 1795, John Keats was an English Romantic poet and author of several poems, three of which are considered to be among the finest in the English language.

Response: Send John Keats a message as he stands on the shore of the wide world.
(Extend your learning: If you were on a walk with him, what would you say?)

©2010, 2017. Wheaton Press™ All Rights Reserved.

A Closer look at Authentic Materialism

"The Madman"
Friedrich Nietzsche

The Madman—Have you not heard of that madman who lit a lantern in the bright morning hours, ran to the market place, and cried incessantly: "I seek God! I seek God!"—As many of those who did not believe in God were standing around just then, he provoked much laughter. Has he got lost? Asked one. Did he lose his way like a child? Asked another. Or is he hiding? Is he afraid of us? Has he gone on a voyage? Emigrated?—Thus they yelled and laughed.

The madman jumped into their midst and pierced them with his eyes. "Whither is God?" he cried; "I will tell you. We have killed him – you and I. All of us are his murderers. But how did we do this? How could we drink up the sea? Who gave us the sponge to wipe away the entire horizon? What were we doing when we unchained this earth from its sun? Whither is it moving now? Whither are we moving? Away from all suns? Are we not plunging continually? Backward, sideward, forward, in all directions? Is there still any up or down? Are we not straying as through an infinite nothing? Do we not feel the breath of empty space? Has it not become colder? Is not night continually closing in on us? Do we not need to light the lanterns in the morning? Do we hear nothing as yet of the noise of the gravediggers who are burying God? Do we smell nothing as yet of the divine decomposition? Gods, too, decompose. God is dead. God remains dead. And we have killed him.

"How shall we comfort ourselves, the murderers of all murderers? What was holiest and mightiest of all that the world has yet owned has bled to death under our knives: who will wipe this blood off us? What water is there for us to clean ourselves? What festivals of atonement, what sacred games shall we have to invent? Is not the greatness of this deed too great for us? Must we ourselves not become gods simply to appear worthy of it? There has never been a greater deed; and whoever is born after us—for the sake of this deed he will belong to a higher history than all history hitherto."

Here the madman fell silent and looked again at his listeners; and they, too, were silent and stared at him in astonishment. At last he threw his lantern on the ground, and it broke into pieces and went out. "I have come too early," he said then; "my time is not yet. This tremendous event is still on its way, still wandering; it has not yet reached the ears of men. Lightning and thunder require time to be seen and heard. This deed is still more distant from them than the most distant stars—and yet they have done it themselves."

It has been related further that on the same day the madman forced his way into several churches and there struck up his *requiem aeternam deo*. Led out and called to account, he is said always to have replied nothing but: "What after all are these churches now if they are not the tombs and sepulchers of God?"

A special shout out of deep gratitude to my friend and colleague David Chase for this translation and the permission to print it here.

 ©2010, 2017. Wheaton Press™ All Rights Reserved.

A Closer look at Authentic Materialism
The Madman

Read and annotate the short translation of Friedrich Nietzsche's famous short essay "The Madman" provided in the workbook.

What is your personal emotional response to Nietzsche's essay? How do you feel after reading this?

Work in small groups to find three things a "hard core" authentic materialist could tweet from this essay:

#madman

Tweet #1:

Tweet #2:

Tweet #3:

Who is the Madman in the story?

Artwork courtesy of Princess Allison Spoelhof

©2010, 2017. Wheaton Press™ All Rights Reserved.

A Closer Look at Authentic Materialism
Chesterton and "The Madman"

1. Discussion Question: What could you imagine G.K. Chesterton saying in response to this essay considering the title of Chapter 2 in his book *Orthodoxy* is entitled "The Maniac"? Why do you think that the general atheistic movement has attached itself to the quote "god is dead"?

   Explanation:

   Explain this in the context of "god" being simply a concept, idea, or an objective philosophical ideal or standard.

   Explain this in the context of "god" being the God of the Holy Bible or even specifically the Hebrew man named Jesus.

2. Discussion Question: Considering that Christians believe that Jesus is God, that God actually died at a certain point in human history, and could say "god is dead" along with Nietzsche, would it be more effective for the general modern atheist movement to adopt a new slogan from this essay "god remains dead"?

3. Optional Project: Design a new bumper sticker or t-shirt of the new slogan for a new atheist movement pulled from the essay.

Artwork courtesy of Princess Allison Spoelhof

 ©2010, 2017. Wheaton Press™ All Rights Reserved.

Scripture Reading Integrity Assignments
Ecclesiastes and materialism

In one sitting, read and annotate these potent words to the citizens of the kingdom of Israel during the reign of King Solomon. Imagine you are a citizen of Solomon's glorious kingdom where he reigns as an aging king after gaining the reputation as one blessed with divine wisdom from the almighty, true God. Where do you see connections to our discussion on materialism and the believers, ways, and "isms" that base their Trust List on this philosophical approach to reality? The connections you make can be subtle, overt, literary, historical, artistic, personal, or metaphoric.

In the space below, write down at least three verses that you find engaging, and briefly explain why you picked these verses. Cut and paste or write out the entire verse, but do not simply put the reference. Do not summarize the verse as a response.

©2010, 2017. Wheaton Press™ All Rights Reserved.

A Closer Look at Complete Monism

We use what we trust to formulate our conclusions concerning the nature of reality.

MONISM (Pantheism):   We are already part of "god" (the Universe); embrace and enjoy this truth and stop striving to become what you already are.

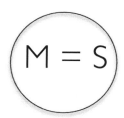

Artwork public domain

Complete Monists trust that both the measurable Material and mysterious Spiritual realms co-exist as one (very large) entity. Monists, often called Pan-Theists, assert that ALL of Reality is One Reality presenting itself as "dual" in Nature; this duality is represented in unlimited perspectives and polarities as experienced throughout the vast complexity and tensions of life. While humans tend to perceive reality as separated, Monists assert that these distinctions are a deception. Due to the perception of separateness Monism is often expressed as or interpreted as "Dualism" because the polarities inherent in Monism tend to manifest as perceived necessary opposites like good and evil or light and dark. For a Complete Monist, all of life is connected literally. Humans are part of all existence, and all of that which exists is already the Ideal for life and thus is already perfect as various parts of the one entity that Monists often refer to as "god." God literally is everything and humans are part of the everything that exists. For all of Life: Emotions = Spirit = God = Truth = Life = Material = Perspective = Emotions. Like a human body which has many apparent distinctions and parts yet maintains a complex unity and harmony, so is the Universal Reality and Unity of Monism. Humans each embody (literally) unique perspectives of god; Humans have unlimited potential and power as god or as a connected part of god. Humans can embrace their unique preferences and seek a balance of all perspectives and polarities so as to wake up, realize, and utilize their true identity and literal unity. Humans (along with all creatures and all parts of reality) can grow in awareness of all perspectives as they embody the simplicity and complexities of life as part of the one (gigantic) self. Humans can learn how to see all of life and all of life's tensions and polarities—the dualities of life—as a valid and valuable part of humanity's oneness, collective unity, and coexistence with all that exists.

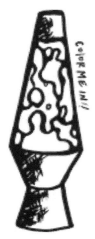

76   ©2010, 2017. Wheaton Press™ All Rights Reserved.

COMPLETE MONISM: Reality Check, Research, Religions, Relevancy, Recognition…

Cultural Connections:

Poetry and Books:

Film:

Music:

Religion:

Sacred Texts:

Historical Figures:

Influential/Famous People:

Key Landmarks/Historical Significance:

©2010, 2017. Wheaton Press™ All Rights Reserved.

A Closer Look at Complete Monism

Learning Assessment
"The Egg"

Read the poem "The Egg" by Andy Weir. Write a personal Reader Response to this unique piece of writing. Traditional Reader Response is in two parts. First, give your immediate response to what you read. Second, give an analytical response to why you think you responded the way you initially did to the piece of writing.

Part 1: Your initial personal emotional response.

Part 2: Your thoughtful, reflective, and analytical small group response.

 ©2010, 2017. Wheaton Press™ All Rights Reserved.

Scripture Reading Integrity Assignments
I John and Monism

Read and annotate I John, the letter written by the Apostle John, as an essay in one sitting.

Pretend you are hearing it for the first time just years after Jesus has come back from the dead.

Where do you see connections to our discussion on monism and the religions, ways, and "isms" that base their Trust List on this philosophical approach to reality?

The connections you make can be subtle, overt, literary, historical, artistic, personal, or metaphoric.

In the space below, write down at least three verses that you find engaging, and briefly explain why you picked these verses. Cut and paste or write out the entire verse, but do not simply put the reference. Do not summarize the verse as a response.

Photo courtesy of Prince Joel Swick

A Closer Look at Religious Theism

We use what we trust to formulate our conclusions concerning the nature of reality.

RELIGIOUS THEISM (Monotheism): We are unique individual creations hoping to become perfect (or complete) so as to dwell with God our Perfect Creator.

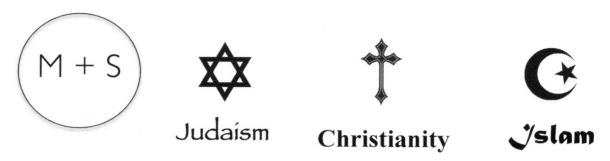

Judaism   Christianity   Islam

Religious Theists trust that both the Spiritual and the Material are components of Prime Reality, and while they are interdependent and dependent with one another, they are also mysteriously intradependent, dependent within each other. Humans are unique individual creations in the image of a free, independent, personal, and all-powerful Creator often referred to as God. Although Humans are created in the image of The One Perfect God, as individual distinct creations of God, Humans are actually independent beings from God and do not possess the exact nature of God. Humans are created to dwell freely with God and enjoy a relationship with God and God's creation. On earth Humans exist as imperfect (incomplete) beings, essentially separated from God's perfect identity and standards. Therefore, in order for Humans to escape eternal separation from their Perfect Creator and to dwell perpetually with their Perfect Creator, individual perfection (fullness) must be achieved and sustained.

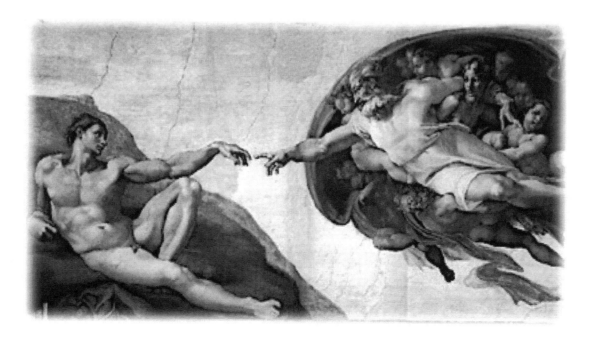

     ©2010, 2017. Wheaton Press™ All Rights Reserved.

RELIGIOUS THEISM: Reality Check, Research, Religions, Relevancy, Recognition...

Cultural Connections:

Poetry and Books:

Film:

Music:

Religion:

Sacred Texts:

Historical Figures:

Influential/Famous People:

Key Landmarks/Historical Significance:

A Closer Look at Religious Theism
A discussion on "I Love You and Buddha Too"
Listen to or watch the Mason Jennings's song "I love you and Buddha to" on YouTube.

1. There is a lot of love mentioned here. What do you believe is the chief goal or purpose of this declaration and all the various kinds of love mentioned in this song? Write down some of the "catchy lines" in this song? *The purpose of all the love is to mothed all the religion are filled virtlug To Lae you gvil and come to you.*

2. The main question in this song is, "Why do some people say there is just one way?"

   - What are various potential answers to this bold question?
     Recouse Most people believed in only one religion
   - What is your personal answer to this question?

   - Who are the "some people" the narrator is referring to?

   - What are some of the answers that "some people" are known to give?

3. In his Gospel, the Apostle John quotes Jesus as saying a very bold statement: "I am the way, the truth, and the life. No one comes to the Father except through me" (John 14:6, NIV).

   1. Why is this considered a controversial and exclusive claim?

   2. What new philosophical insights are gained or lost by interpreting the words "the Father" to mean "perfection"?

   3. Why *philosophically* and *theologically* is this statement not rude or exclusive?

   4. What are the implications if a false translation of Jesus' statement were published as "I am a way, but there are other valid ways. I am a truth among many truths. I am a form of life. Anyone can get to the Father or achieve perfection however they so choose, but I am a pretty good option"?

 ©2010, 2017. Wheaton Press™ All Rights Reserved.

"Discerning the Spirits"
Quotes, notes, doodles, and discussion

"The Inch" and the "Crazy Arm Thing": Human Spirit & Holy Spirit

Photo public domain

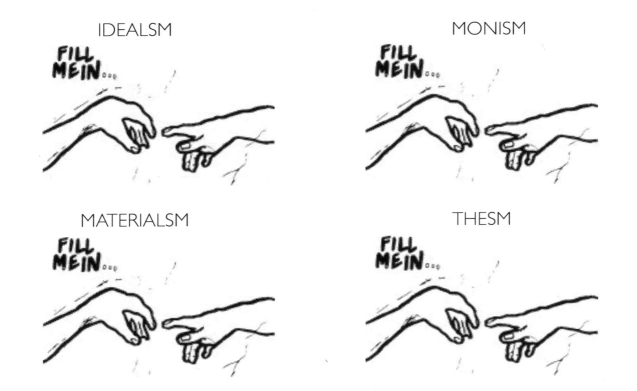

©2010, 2017. Wheaton Press™ All Rights Reserved. 83

Scripture Reading Integrity Assignments
The Gospel of John and theism

Read and annotate the Gospel of John as a long essay in one sitting. Pretend you are hearing this for the first time as a true story about the man Jesus. Where do you see connections to our discussion on theism, especially the religions, ways, "isms," and those with a "religious spirit" that base their Trust List on this philosophical approach to reality? The connections you make can be subtle, overt, literary, historical, artistic, personal, or metaphoric.

In the space below, write down at least three verses that you find engaging, and briefly explain why you picked these verses. Cut and paste or write out the entire verse, but do not simply put the reference. Do not summarize the verse as a response.

Artwork courtesy of Princess Olivia Age 3

 ©2010, 2017. Wheaton Press™ All Rights Reserved.

Unit 3
(ACT 3)

Paradox &
The Fullness of
Reality

Philosophy & Theology
INVITED TO TRUST

UNIT 3 (Act 3) ESSENTIAL QUESTIONS:

1. What is *Perichoresis as a World View*?
2. How can I use Lewis's Moral Argument in Book one of Mere Christianity to come to a trustworthy God-Centered world view.
3. Why is Jesus essential to an authentic Trinitarian (Perichoresis) World View.
4. How can I use Lewis's Book Two of Mere Christianity to come to a trustworthy Christ-Centered world view.
5. What is authentic Biblical Grace and Salvation through Grace; and what makes Grace so unique in the contexts of the fractured version of the four world views?
6. Why is Grace connected to Jesus and a Christ-Centered World view?
7. Why is Jesus' way to live the best way to live?

UNIT 3 (Act 3) READINGS:

1. Chesterton, G.K. *Orthodoxy* (Chapter 6)
2. Lewis, C.S. *Mere Christianity* Book 1
3. Lewis, C.S. *Mere Christianity* Book 2
4. *Romans*

UNIT 3 (Act 3) THINKBOOK LEARNING OPPORTUNITIES:

Formative:

❑ Annotations and Analytical Reader Response: "Paradoxes of Christianity"
❑ Annotations and Analytical Reader Response: *Mere Christianity* (Book 1)
❑ Annotations and Analytical Reader Response: *Mere Christianity* (Book 2)
❑ Scripture Reading "Truth Revealed": *Romans* and *Mere Christianity* (Book 1 & 2)

Summative:
❑ A Midway Project: On Philosophy, The four World Views, Mere Christianity, and Orthodoxy

UNIT 3 (Act 3) LEARNING PLAN:

1. Paradoxes of Christianity
2. An Introduction to *Mere Christianity*
2. *Mere Christianity* (Book 1)
3. *Mere Christianity* (Book 2)
4. Book of Romans
5. Parable of Grace

 ©2010, 2017. Wheaton Press™ All Rights Reserved.

Silly Strips

The Trust List: The Fullness of Christ
A Christ-centered incarnational worldview

"There is a huge and heroic sanity of which moderns can only collect the fragments. There is a giant of whom we see only the lopped arms and legs walking about.

They have torn the soul of Christ into silly strips,

Labeled egoism and altruism, and they are equally puzzled by his insane magnificence and his insane meekness.

They have parted his garments among them, and for his vesture they have cast lots; though the coat was without seam woven from the top throughout."

G. K. Chesterton (Orthodoxy, "Suicide of Thought")

- What are the "silly strips" Chesterton refers to?

- What silly strips are you holding onto?

- Can you think of a friend or colleague who is clinging to a single strip, thinking it's the whole picture.

On your own:
Draw a picture of the shards of the sword, "Narsil," form the Lord of the Rings as a metaphor for truth!

Upon examination, one can see this is a complete sword, just broken into many shards. Each piece on it's own isn't completely trustworthy, or particularly useful, but is an authentic part of the whole, original "Narsil." This can be a potent visual representation of a fractured worldview.
This metaphor can also represent anytime we use Scripture and Prophecy (The Sword of the Spirit which is the Word of God) out of context and fracture the Truth contained.

The Last Supper
Quotes, notes, doodles, and discussion

We have cut up the masterpiece

But it is still a piece of the "original"

Photo public domain

 ©2010, 2017. Wheaton Press™ All Rights Reserved.

The Chandelier Metaphor

If you take the diagram below and pretend that you could hold it above your head, it would appear like a chandelier. The chandelier is a visual representation of how all four worldviews intermingle and, through paradox, create the area for Truth to exist. There are apparent opposites on each side that create space in which each concept operates. For example, notice "objectivity" and its opposite "relativity" – the two must balance one another for Truth to be expressed. The same is true for "unity" and "distinction." This diagram describes all four circles intermingling and balancing one another – this is the expression of a complete, balanced truth. Remember, there will be tension between the seeming opposites. However, when we try to resolve that tension we will lose the Truth found in the balance between the truths.

As you turn the individual "lights" of the chandelier on and off, different perspectives or worldviews are revealed. Let's take a look at how that works. Remember that one of the keys to the truth embedded within this metaphor is that the sum of the whole is greater then the parts combined.

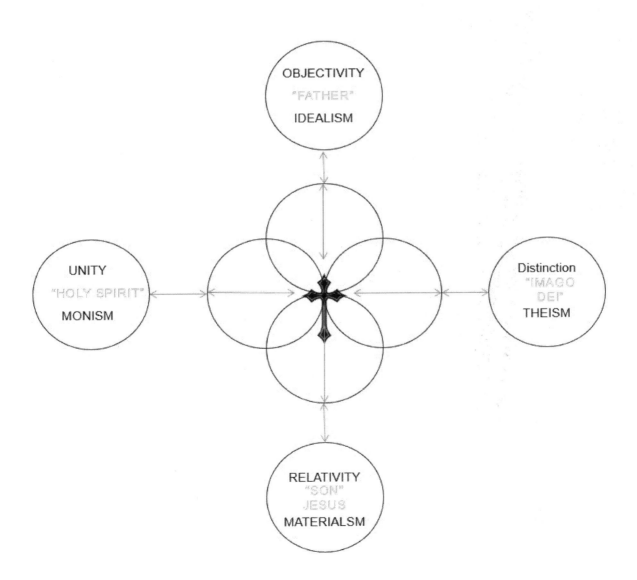

©2010, 2017. Wheaton Press™ All Rights Reserved.

The Chandelier Metaphor On/Off Switch

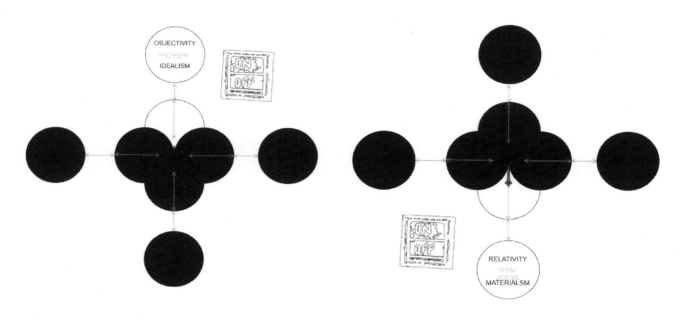

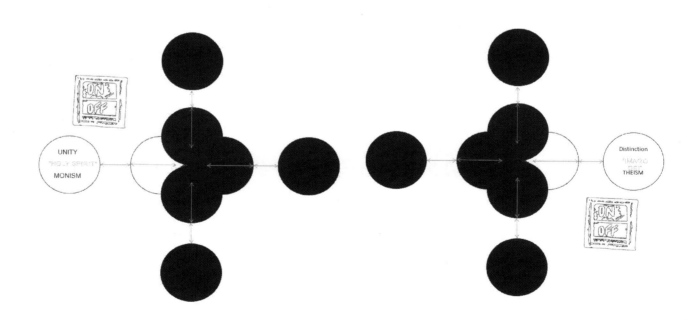

 ©2010, 2017. Wheaton Press™ All Rights Reserved.

The Chandelier Metaphor

- What are some key consequences for turning out the lights on idealism?

- What are some key consequences for turning out the lights on materialism?

- What are some key consequences for turning out the lights on monism?

- What are some key consequences for turning out the lights on theism?

- What are some potential lights you have turned off on your own journey?

©2010, 2017. Wheaton Press™ All Rights Reserved. 91

The Chandelier Metaphor

The main goal of this scene was to create a repository of information to start or continue conversations on the real and often potent consequences of the various trust lists.

This is an organic, but not exhaustive list of the complexities of the costs and the benefits of trusting various answers to the big seven questions used in this book. It is meant to be thought-provoking and conversation worthy; feel free to disagree, debate, dialogue, discuss, and differentiate. This type of information is helpful when you are trying to figure out what you believe or to start the journey of understanding why someone else might have a different answer on their trust list than the one on yours. Everybody trusts something. Of course, there is a cost to that choice, but of course there are benefits as well—otherwise no human would trust it. In our conversation with people of different worldviews, many people see only the negatives of the other side. It can be invaluable to look for the benefits in other options and trust lists as you assess your own.

All of life is a journey, and we are all at different places on our journey. Much of the adventure is filled with perpetually learning how to renew our minds and learning how to think differently. It all starts with learning how to trust something and even Someone new, not just with our heads but also with our hearts, and ultimately with our whole beings. This takes time, dialogue, thoughtful contemplation, surrender, outside help, and the vital process of being on the journey of a lifetime.

Here is one of my favorite, and for the content of this text, one of the most poignant quotes from C.S. Lewis[2]. I place it here because of the potent implications of inviting Jesus into your philosophical house and adding this living Being, who happens to be the Creator and sustainer of your soul and the universe, to your personal trust list.

"Imagine yourself as a living house. God comes in to rebuild that house. At first, perhaps, you can understand what He is doing. He is getting the drains right and stopping the leaks in the roof and so on; you knew that those jobs needed doing and so you are not surprised. But presently He starts knocking the house about in a way that hurts abominably and does not seem to make any sense. What on earth is He up to? The explanation is that He is building quite a different house from the one you thought of - throwing out a new wing here, putting on an extra floor there, running up towers, making courtyards. You thought you were being made into a decent little cottage: but He is building a palace. He intends to come and live in it Himself."

 ©2010, 2017. Wheaton Press™ All Rights Reserved.

Paradox and Oxymoron
Quotes, notes, doodles, and discussion

Paradox is essentially about the matter of balancing the opposites of the truth you wish to describe – thus creating a space in which that particular Truth resides.

Paradox is the living fibers that weave and hold the Truth together is beautiful tension and strength.

If you are not living in the tension of paradox you may not be living WITHIN the Truth.

Some Quotes from "Paradoxes of Christianity" Orthodoxy, Ch. 6 (Chesterton)

"The real trouble with this world of ours is not that it is an unreasonable world, nor even that it is a reasonable one. The commonest kind of trouble is that it is nearly reasonable, but not quite. Life is not an illogicality; yet it is a trap for logicians."

"Paganism declared that virtue was in a balance; Christianity declared it was in a conflict: the collision of two passions apparently opposite. Of course they were not really inconsistent; but they were such that it was hard to hold simultaneously."

"Courage is almost a contradiction in terms. It means a strong desire to live taking the form of a readiness to die. 'He that will lose his life, the same shall save it,' is not a piece of mysticism for saints and heroes. It is a piece of everyday advice for sailors or mountaineers. It might be printed in an Alpine guide or a drill book. This paradox is the whole principle of courage; even of quite earthly or quite brutal courage."

Richard Rhor: "Paradox as Endless Knowability"
Weekly Summary of devotionals on paradox August 2017

The binary, dualistic mind cannot deal with contradictions, paradox, or mystery, all of which are at the heart of religion. (Sunday)

The very nature of spiritual truth is that it is paradoxical. (Monday)

The times where we meet or reckon with our contradictions are often turning points, opportunities to enter into the deeper mystery of God or, alternatively, to evade the mystery of God. (Tuesday)

If you hold both sides seriously, that is the space in which you can grow morally, in understanding what really matters. That is the space in which you can go deep and learn mystery—which is endlessly knowability. (Wednesday)

The third way is not balancing or even eliminating the opposites, but holding the opposites, as Jesus did on the cross. To live inside this space of creative tension is the very character of faith, hope, and love. (Thursday)

[This third way that Christ Models for us is what Rhor calls a] "Third Force" energy is overcoming seeming opposites by uncovering a reconciling third that is bigger than both of the parts and doesn't exclude either of them. (Friday)

©2010, 2017. Wheaton Press™ All Rights Reserved.

"PARADOXES & OXYMORONS": Quotes & Notes, Doodles and Discussion:

THE POWER OF PARADOX

Lion   T   L a m b
Justice   R   M e r c y
Simple   U   C o m p l e x
Fully God   T   F u l l y   M a n
Grace   H   W o r k s
Free Will   God Ordained
Alpha   Omega

-   -
-   -
-   -
-   -
-   -
-   -
-   -
-   -

Artwork courtesy of Princess Allison Spoelhof

 ©2010, 2017. Wheaton Press™ All Rights Reserved.

Mere Christianity
Preface, Book 1

A Few Opening Quotes to Set the Stage for Discussion

Foreword: (Kathleen Norris)
"The Christianity Lewis espouses is humane, but not easy; it asks us to recognize that the great religious struggle is not fought on a spectacular battle ground, but within the ordinary human heart, when every morning we awake and feel the pressures of the day crowding in on us, we must decide what sort of immortals we wish to be" p. XX

"As Lewis reminds us, with his customary humor and wit, 'How monotonously alike all the great tyrants and conquerors have been; how gloriously different the saints'" p. XX

"There are no ordinary people. It is immortals whom we joke with, work with, marry, snob, exploit" The Weight of Glory, a sermon delivered by C. S. Lewis in 1941

Preface
"One of the things Christians are disagreed about is the importance of their disagreements" p. X

Christian: "One who accepts the common doctrines of Christianity" p. XII
See James Sire's "The Universe Next Door" handout

"It is not for us to say who, in the deepest sense, is or is not close to the spirit of Christ. We do not see into men's hearts. We cannot judge, and are indeed forbidden to judge. It would be wicked arrogance for us to say that a man is, or is not, a Christian in this refined sense" p. XIV

"The name Christians was first given at Antioch (Acts 11:26) to 'the disciples', to those who accepted the teaching of the apostles....When a man who accepts the Christian doctrine lives unworthily of it, is much clearer to say he is a bad Christian than to say he is not a Christian" p. XV

Discussion Notes:

"It ['mere' Christianity] is more like a hall out of which doors open into several rooms. If I can bring anyone into that hall, I have done what I attempted. But it is in the rooms, not in the hall, that there are fires and chairs and meals. The hall is a place to wait in, a place from which to try the various doors, not a place to live in" p. XV

"You must keep on praying for the light: and, of course, even in the hall, you must begin trying to obey the rules common to the whole house" p. XVI

"When you have reached your own room, be kind to those who have chosen different doors and to those who are still in the hall. If they are wrong they need your prayers all the more; and if they are your enemies, then you are under orders to pray for them. That is one of the rules common to the whole house" p. XVI

Discussion Notes:

Mere Christianity: The Moral Argument for the Existence of God

Concept Map for Book I

Foreword (Kathleen Norris)

"The Christianity Lewis espouses is humane, but not easy; it asks us to recognize that the great religious struggle is not fought on a spectacular battle ground, but within the ordinary human heart, when every morning we awake and feel the pressures of the day crowding in on us, we must decide what sort of immortals we wish to be." (pg. XX)

The argument's premises

Premise #1: "First, that human beings, all over the earth, have this curious idea that they ought to behave in a certain way, and cannot get rid of it." (pg. 8)

Premise #2: "Secondly, that they do not in fact behave in that way. They know the Law of Nature; they break it." (pg. 8)

Premise #3: "Consequently, this Rule of Right and Wrong, or Law of Human Nature, or whatever you call it, must somehow be a real thing – a thing that is really there, not made up by ourselves. And yet it is not a fact in the ordinary sense, in the same way as our actual behavior is a fact. It begins to look as if we shall have to admit that there is more than one kind of reality; that, in this particular case, there is something above and beyond the ordinary facts of men's behavior, and yet quite definitely real – a real law, which none of us made, but we find pressing on us." (pg. 20)

Premise #4: "There is 'something which is directing the universe, and which appears in me as a law urging me to do right and making me feel responsible and uncomfortable when I do wrong." (pg. 25)

Premise #5: This is the terrible fix we are in. If the universe is not governed by an absolute goodness, then all of our efforts are in the long run hopeless. But if it is, then we are making ourselves enemies to that goodness every day, and are not in the least likely to do any better tomorrow, and so our case is hopeless again. We cannot do with it, and we cannot do without it." (pg. 31)

Premise #6: Of course, I quite agree that the Christian religion is, in the long run, a thing of unspeakable comfort. But it does not begin in comfort, it begins in the dismay I have been describing, and it is no use at all trying to go on to that comfort without first going through that dismay." (pg. 32)

Conclusion of Book 1: "Christianity tells people to repent and promises them forgiveness. It therefore has nothing (as far as I know) to say to people who do not know that they need any forgiveness. It is after you have realized that there is a Moral Law, and a Power behind the law, and that you have broken that law and put yourself wrong with that Power—it is after all of this, and not a moment sooner, that Christianity begins to talk." (pg. 31)

Mere Christianity: The Moral Argument for the Existence of God

Concept Map for Book 1

Summarize these ideas in your own words:

Premise #1: _why God who every thing in world_

"First…

Premise #2: _pick_

"Second…

Premise #3:

"Consequently…

Premise #4:

"There is…

Premise #5:

"This is…

Premise #6:

"Of course…

Conclusion of Book 1:

"Christianity…

©2010, 2017. Wheaton Press™ All Rights Reserved.

Mere Christianity, Book 1, Chapter 1: Concept Map for Book 1

BOOK I: Right and wrong as a clue to the meaning of the universe
(Bold and italics are added By Mr. D. for emphasis)

Chapter 1. The Law of Nature

"He is appealing to some kind of standard of behavior which he expects the other man to know about. And the other man very seldom replies: 'To hell with your standard.' Nearly always he tries to make out that what he has been doing does not really go against the standard, or that if it does there is some special excuse." (pg. 3)

"Quarreling means trying to show that the other man is in the wrong. And there would be no sense in trying to do that unless you and he had some sort of agreement as to what Right and Wrong are; just as there would be no sense in saying that a footballer had committed a foul unless there was some agreement about the rules of football." (pg. 4)

"We may put this another way. Each man is at every moment subjected to several different sets of law but there is only one of these which he is free to disobey." (pg. 4) *Therefore, we cannot disobey the law of gravity.*

"But the most remarkable thing is this. Whenever you find a man who says he does not believe in a real Right and Wrong, you will find the same man going back on this a moment later. He may break his promise to you, but if you try breaking one to him he will be complaining 'It's not fair' before you can say Jack Robinson." (pg. 6)
Generally, for a relativist, there will be a breaking point when they will say STOP if you were to really push relativity to its extreme. Most people, unless they are a true atheist, when pushed to totally believe the consequences of true relativity (absurdity and absolute moral license), they are not willing to stake their personal possessions, life, or family on it because when anything does go, they can't say it's not fair. But this statement can't be said because they would be appealing to an objective standard for morality which would nullify relativity!

Therefore: "It seems, then, we are forced to believe in a real Right and Wrong." (pg. 7)

"Now if we are agreed about that, I go on to my next point, which is this. None of us are really keeping the Law of Nature. If there are any exceptions among you, I apologize to them. They had better read some other book, for nothing I am going to say concerns them. And now, turning to the ordinary human beings that are left" (pg. 7)

"I am only trying to call attention to a fact; that fact that this year, or this month, or, more likely this very day, we have failed to practice ourselves the kind of behavior we expect from other people. There may be all sorts of excuses." (pg. 7)

"The question at the moment is not whether they are good excuses. The point is that they are one more proof of how deeply, whether we like it or not, we believe in the Law of Nature. If we do not believe in decent behavior, why should we be so anxious to make excuses for not having behaved decently? …[W]e cannot bear to face the fact that we are breaking it, and consequently we try to shift the responsibility." (pg. 8)
People want to avoid responsibility and consequences for their mistakes or wrong behavior.

Premise #1: "First, that human beings, all over the earth, have this curious idea that they ought to behave in a certain way, and cannot get rid of it." (pg. 8)

Premise #2: "Secondly, that they do not in fact behave in that way. They know the Law of Nature; they break it." (pg. 8)

"These two facts are the foundation of all clear thinking about ourselves and the universe we live in." (pg. 8)
Note: Lewis calls them facts.

 ©2010, 2017. Wheaton Press™ All Rights Reserved.

Mere Christianity, Book 1, Chapter 2: Concept Map for Book 1

Chapter 2. Some objections

(Bold and italics are added By Mr. D. for emphasis)

1) "Isn't what you call the Moral Law simply our herd instinct and hasn't it been developed just like our other instincts?" (pg. 9) *Thanks to much of Richard Dawkins' work this has now shifted into a conversation on Genetic Theory.*
"But feeling a desire to help [based on our instincts] is quite different from feeling you ought to help whether you want to or not. Supposing you hear a cry for help from a man in danger. You will probably feel two desires—one desire to give help (due to your herd instinct), the other a desire to keep out of danger (due to the instinct of self preservation). But you will find inside of you, in addition to these two impulses, a third thing which tells you that you ought to follow the impulse to help, and suppress the impulse to run away. Now this thing that judges between the instincts, that decides which should be encouraged, cannot itself be either of them." (pg. 9-10)
Can we admit that we have a sense of what we ought to do?—that sense of "ought to" is different than what we are deciding between doing; it is what is deciding the actions not the actions themselves, and it is what propels or inhibits what we do.

"If two instincts are in conflict, and there is nothing in a creature's mind except those instincts, obviously the stronger of the two must win." (pg. 10) *But that is not so. See his examples on pages 10 and 11*
" If the moral law was one of our instincts, we ought to be able to point to some one impulse inside us which was always what we call 'good', always in agreement with the rule of right behavior. But you cannot. [*Here is where relativity tries to get some of its weight and authority.*] Think once again of the piano. It has not got two kinds of notes on it, the 'right' notes and the 'wrong' ones. Every single note is right at one time and wrong at another." (pg. 11)
The notes are likened to various instincts in this analogy, and atheism and romanticism feed off this idea of living as though there is no standard for a tune of morality; but this is not so.

Therefore: "The Moral Law is not any one instinct or set of instincts: it is something which makes a kind of tune by directing the instincts." (pg. 11) *The moral law is the standard that tells us which instincts to act on and when to act on them.*

2) "Isn't what you call the Moral Law just a social convention, something that is put into us by education?" (pg. 12)
"But some of the things we learn are mere conventions which might have been different—we learn to keep to the left of the road, but it might just as well have been the rule to keep to the right—and others of them, like mathematics, are real truths. The question is to which class the Law of Human Nature belongs." (pg. 12)

    A. "Though there are differences between the moral ideas of one time or country and those of another, the differences are not very great… and you can recognize the same law running through them all: whereas mere conventions, like the rule of the road or the kind of clothes people wear, may differ to any extent". (pg. 12)
    *Please see the end of The Abolition of Man handout where Lewis gives concrete examples of this cross - historical and cross-cultural morality.

    B. "When you think about these differences between the morality of one people and another, do you think that the morality of one people is ever better or worse than that of another?" (pg. 13)
    We can't really do this with driving or clothes, but we can with morality.

It follows then that: "The moment you say that one set of moral ideals can be better than another, you are, in fact, measuring them both by a standard, saying that one of them conforms to that standard more nearly than the other. But the standard that measures the two things is something different from either." (pg. 13)

Therefore: "You are, in fact, comparing them both with some Real Morality, admitting that there is such a thing as a real Right, independent of what people think, and that some people's ideas get nearer to that real Right than others." (pg. 13)
He points to the definition of an absolute—any being entity or idea that exists "independent of what people think."

©2010, 2017. Wheaton Press™ All Rights Reserved.

Mere Christianity, **Book 1, Chapter 3:** Concept Map for Book 1

Interestingly, when you discuss chapters 1 and 2 with a true relativist (atheist or romantic), it often helps them (and you) define the true nature of what they really believe. **Without an absolute standard for morality—outside of human convention—anything goes!** *And that is truly terrifying to most people.*

Chapter 3. The reality of the law
(Bold and italics are added By Mr. D. for emphasis)

"Two odd things about the human race" (pg. 16)
Premise (#1 again): "First, that they were haunted by the idea of a sort of behavior they ought to practice, what you might call fair play, or decency, or morality, or the Law of Nature."
Premise (#2 again): "Second, that they did not in fact do so." (pg. 16)

"After all, you may say, what I call breaking the Law of Right and Wrong or of Nature, only means that people are not perfect. And why on earth should I expect them to be?" (pg. 16)
Here, Lewis does many things at once: He builds his current argument on the objectivity of the moral law, and he subtly sets up the fact that if we will admit to being imperfect, what will we do when we are faced with the fact that in order to ultimately be right with God (who, by definition, is good and perfect), we need to be holy (or perfect)? This sets up our need for Christ, the only one who can make us holy before God. Also, note his creativity and wit in saying, "why on earth should I expect them to be"— this is a heavenly expectation!

"I am trying to find out truth. And from that point of view the very idea of something being imperfect, of its not being what it ought to be, has certain consequences." (pg. 16)
See his examples on pages 16-17.

Clarification: "The laws of nature, as applied to stones or trees, may only mean 'what Nature, in fact, does'. But if you turn to the Law of Human Nature, the Law of Decent Behavior, it is a different matter. That law certainly does not mean 'what human beings, in fact do'; for as I said before, many of them do not obey this law at all, and none of them obey it completely. The law of gravity tells you what stones do if you drop them; but the Law of Human Nature tells you what human beings ought to do and not do. In other words, when you are dealing with humans, something else comes in above and beyond the actual facts." (pg. 17)

Another Clarification: Decent behavior is a matter of convenience to me and to others: "But that is simply untrue. A man occupying the corner seat in the train because he got there first, and a man who slipped into it while my back was turned and removed my bag, are both equally inconvenient. But I blame the second man and do not blame the first." (pg. 18)
* *See the rest of his examples: "And as for decent behavior in ourselves, [being convenient], I suppose it is pretty obvious that it does not mean the behavior that pays [that is rewarding or convenient]. It means things like being content with thirty shillings when you might have got three pounds, doing school work honestly when it would be easy to cheat, leaving a girl alone when you would like to make love to her, staying in dangerous places when you would rather go somewhere safer, keeping promises you would rather not keep, and telling the truth even when it makes you look like a fool." (pg. 17)*

Another Clarification: *In the middle of page 17, Lewis talks about the fact that the only way for society to be truly safe and happy is for people to be "honest and fair and kind to each other." But he makes the important subtle distinction that this misses his point. Explaining how to behave rightly is circular, Lewis is explaining why we ought to behave in a certain way and why all people appeal to this sense of ought to as why to behave that certain way. He gives another example of it on the top of page 20; he also builds his argument to another climax on the last half of page 20.*

Premise # 3: "Consequently, this Rule of Right and Wrong, or Law of Human Nature, or whatever you call it, must somehow be a real thing—a thing that is really there, not made up by ourselves. And yet it is not a fact in the ordinary sense, in the same way as our actual behavior is a fact. It begins to look as if we shall have to admit that there is more than one kind of reality; that, in this particular case, there is something above and beyond the ordinary facts of men's behavior, and yet quite definitely real—a real law, which none of us made, but we find pressing on us." (pg. 20)

 ©2010, 2017. Wheaton Press™ All Rights Reserved.

Mere Christianity, Book 1, Chapter 4: Concept Map for Book 1
Chapter 4. What lies behind the law

Lewis gives a helpful review in the first paragraph on page 21.

> "I now want to consider what this tells us about the universe we live in. Ever sense men were able to think they have been wondering what this universe really is and how it came to be there. And very roughly, two views have been held." (pg. 21)

"First there is the materialist view. People who take this view think that matter and space just happen to exist, and always have existed, nobody knows why; and the matter, behaving in certain fixed ways, just happened to be a fluke, to produce creatures like ourselves who are able to think." P. 21 *He goes on to explain how, according to a materialist, everything is a matter of "chance" (pg. 21)*
This is the atheistic existentialist view. Think Frankenstein: Matter and electricity are all we are and ever will be. Therefore, chance, true random chance, is the fundamental way to explain personal experiences; thus all experiences, positive or negative, are void of lasting purpose, direction, or meaning.

"The other view is the religious view. According to it, what is behind the universe is more like a mind than it is like anything else we know. That is to say, it is conscious, and has purposes, and prefers one thing to another. And on this view it made the universe, partly for purposes we do not know, but partly, at any rate, in order to produce creatures like itself—I mean, like itself to the extent of having minds." (pg. 22)

Lewis talks about the "romantic" view which is Monism at the core. He calls it the "Life Force view." You can see how it defeats itself in its own circularity and relativity, with a main goal of avoiding pain and consequences for one's actions. See pages 26-27.

"And note this too. You cannot find out which view is the right one by science in the ordinary sense. Science works by experiments. It watches how things behave….But why anything comes to be there at all and whether there is anything behind the things science observes—something of a different kind—this is not a scientific question. If there is 'Something Behind', then either it will have to remain altogether unknown to men or make itself known in a different way, [not in a scientifically measurably way]" (pg. 22-23) *He points us to faith, philosophy, and reason.*

"Now the position would be quite hopeless but for this. There is one thing, and only one, in the whole universe which we could learn about from external observation. That one thing is Man. We do not only observe men, we are men." (pg. 23)
We are what we have to use!

It follows then that: "We have, so to speak, inside information; we are in the know. And because of that we know that men find themselves under a moral law, which they did not make, and cannot quite forget even when they try, and they ought to obey." (pg. 23)
Basically, thus far in this chapter he is pointing out that all we can use to figure out the universe is what we are made of and what we experience, and he lists what we will conclude when we use these things. Remember: Lewis is trying to lead us to the fact that there is an objective Power guiding and ruling the universe; he does so by saying that It can't be us or the universe.

Thus: "If there was a controlling power outside the universe, it could not show itself as one of the facts inside *[or, as]* the universe—no more than the architect of a house could actually be a wall or staircase or fireplace in that house. The only way in which we could expect it to show itself *[so we could validate it—because Lewis just showed us that all we can use to understand the universe is ourselves]* would be inside ourselves as an influence or a command trying to get us to behave in a certain way. And that is just what we do find in ourselves. Surely this ought to arouse our suspicions? *[In a positive, convincing sort of way.]* In the only case where you can expect to get an answer, the answer turns to be Yes; and in other cases where you do not get an answer, you see why you do not. *[Because we ultimately could not personally and honestly validate an answer in any other format, science is not made for this.]*" (pg. 25)

Therefore: Premise # 4: There is "Something which is directing the universe, and which appears in me as a law urging me to do right and making me feel responsible and uncomfortable when I do wrong." (pg. 25)

"I think we have to assume it is more like a mind than it is like anything else we know—because after all, the only other thing we know is matter and you can hardly imagine a bit of matter giving instructions." (pg. 25)

©2010, 2017. Wheaton Press™ All Rights Reserved.

Philosophy & Theology

Mere Christianity, Book 1, Chapter 5: Concept Map for Book 1

Chapter 5. We have cause to be uneasy

"I ended my last chapter with the idea that in the Moral Law somebody or something from beyond the material universe was actually getting at us. . . . You may have felt you were ready to listen to me as long as you thought I had anything new to say; but if it turns out to be only religion, well, the world has tried that and you cannot put the clock back." (pg. 28)
One can't try to turn back time and re-teach what has already failed to work.

First: "And I think if you look at the present state of the world, it is pretty plain that humanity has been making some big mistake. We are on the wrong road. And if that is so, we must go back. Going back is the quickest way on." (pg. 29)
Second: "This has not yet turned into 'religious jaw'. We have not yet got so far as the God of any actual religion, still less the God of that particular religion called Christianity. We have only got as far as a Somebody or Something behind the Moral Law." And "We are not taking anything from the Bible or the Churches; we are trying to see what we can find out about this Somebody on our own steam. And I want to make it quite clear that what we find out on our steam is something that gives us a shock" (pg. 29)
Read Romans; all of it! But, particularly Chapter 1, specifically Chapter 1 verse 20.

We have "two bits of evidence" about this "Somebody or Something behind the Moral Law":
1) "One is the universe he has made." (pg. 29)
2) "The other is that Moral Law which he has put into our minds." (pg. 29)

This: "Now, from this second bit of evidence we conclude that the being behind the universe is intensely interested in right conduct—in fair play, unselfishness, courage, good faith, honesty, and truthfulness." (pg. 30)
He has already brought us to this point in the previous chapters.
Plus this: "There is nothing indulgent about the Moral Law. It is as hard as nails. It tells you to do the straight thing and it does not seem to care how painful, or dangerous, or difficult it is to do so." (pg. 30)
It is objective and absolute—see our notes on the definition of absolute
Clarification: "If it is a pure impersonal mind, there may be no sense in asking it to make allowances for you or let you off, just as there is no sense in asking the multiplication table to let you off, when your sums are wrong" (pg. 30)
Its an Absolute, which will, by definition, demand perfect adherence.
Another clarification: "And it is no use either saying that if there is a God of that sort - an impersonal absolute goodness - then you do not like Him and are not going to bother about Him." (pg. 30)
Arguing with or ignoring an absolute doesn't do any good.
It follows then that: "The trouble is that one part of you is on His side and really agrees with his disapproval of human greed and trickery and exploitation. You may want Him to make an exception in your own case, to let you off this one time; but you know at bottom that unless the Power behind the world really and unalterably detests that sort of behavior, then He cannot be good." (pg. 30)
Lewis wants us to be sure that we get the fact that this absolute Power is Good and detests bad behavior as a part of its nature, being Absolute Goodness.
One more clarification: "We know that if there does exist an absolute goodness it must hate most of what we do." (pg. 31)
Because we do not participate in absolute goodness:, we are depraved. And by definition, Absolute Goodness can have no part in anything less than perfection! We are less than perfect, thus because of our nature we set ourselves apart from this entity.

Therefore: Premise # 5: "This is the terrible fix we are in. If the universe is not governed by an absolute goodness, then all of our efforts are in the long run hopeless. But if it is, then we are making ourselves enemies to that goodness every day, and are not in the least likely to do any better tomorrow, and so our case is hopeless again. **We cannot do with it, and we cannot do without it.**" (pg. 31)

Conclusion of Book I: "Christianity tells people to repent and promises them forgiveness. It therefore has nothing (as far as I know) to say to people who do not know that they need any forgiveness. It is after you have realized that there is a Moral Law, and a Power behind the law, and that you have broken that law and put yourself wrong with that Power – it is after all of this, and not a moment sooner, that Christianity begins to talk." (pg. 31)

Premise # 6: "Of course, I quite agree that the Christian religion is, in the long run, a thing of unspeakable comfort. But it does not begin in comfort it begins in the dismay I have been describing, and it is no use at all trying to go on to that comfort without first going through that dismay." (pg. 32)
We need to know that we are in dire and desperate need of help, mercy, grace, and forgiveness as the beginning and the foundation of our belief system. This is the conclusion of the beginning, and Lewis got here without Scripture or talk of a man named Jesus. He uses simple straightforward logical reasoning and basic philosophy.

Mere Christianity, Book 2: THIS MEANS WAR!

"By the humility and gentleness of Christ, I appeal to you—I, Paul, who am 'timid' when face to face with you, but "bold" toward you when away! I beg you that when I come may not have to be as bold as I expect to be toward some people who think that we live by the standards of this world. For though we live in the world, we do not wage war as the world does. The weapons we fight with are not the weapons of the world. On the contrary, they have divine power to demolish strongholds. We demolish arguments and every pretension that sets itself up against the knowledge of God, and we take captive every thought to make it obedient to Christ."
2 Corinthians 10:1-5 (NIV)

A SHORT LIST of a few of the WEAPONS OF WAR that are not of this world which have DIVINE POWER to demolish strongholds:

- WEAPON #1: *LOVE*

- WEAPON #2: *HONOR*

- WEAPON#3: *GRACE AND TRUTH*

- WEAPON #4: *FORGIVENESS*

- WEAPON #5: *HOPE*

- WEAPON #6: *PARADOX*

- WEAPON #7: *THE WORD OF GOD! EPHESIANS 6*

- WEAPON #8: *JOY*

- WEAPON #9: *FAITH*

READ ISAIAH 61!

DEFINITION OF A STRONGHOLD:
(Keeps people in and Keep people out...)

➤ Spiritual Emotional, Intellectual Stronghold:

➤ Prisoners:

➤ Captives:

©2010, 2017. Wheaton Press™ All Rights Reserved.

Philosophy & Theology

Mere Christianity, Book 2

"By the humility and gentleness of Christ, I appeal to you—I, Paul, who am 'timid' when face to face with you, but "bold" toward you when away! I beg you that when I come may not have to be as bold as I expect to be toward some people who think that we live by the standards of this world. For though we live in the world, we do not wage war as the world does. The weapons we fight with are not the weapons of the world. On the contrary, they have divine power to demolish strongholds. We demolish arguments and every pretension that sets itself up against the knowledge of God, and we take captive every thought to make it obedient to Christ."

2 Corinthians 10:1-5 (NIV)

1. The math equation (pg. 35)

I have been asked to tell you what Christians believe, and I am going to begin by telling you one thing that Christians do not need to believe. If you are a Christian you do not have to believe that all the other religions are simply wrong all through. If you are an atheist you do have to believe that the main point in all the religions of the whole world is simply one huge mistake. If you are a Christian, you are free to think that all these religions, even the queerest ones, contain at least some hint of the truth. When I was an atheist I had to try to persuade myself that most of the human race have always been wrong about the question that mattered to them most; when I became a Christian I was able to take a more liberal view. But, of course, being a Christian does mean thinking that where Christianity differs from other religions, Christianity is right and they are wrong. As in arithmetic-there is only one right answer to a sum, and all other answers are wrong: but some of the wrong answers are much nearer being right than others.

NOTES:

2. MONISM and DUALISM: (pg. 37)

"With this big difference between Pantheism and the Christian idea of God, there usually goes another. Pantheists usually believe that God, so to speak, animates the universe as you animate your body: that the universe almost is God, so that if it did not exist He would not exist either, and anything you find in the universe is a part of God. The Christian idea is quite different. They think God invented and made the universe—like a man making a picture or composing a tune.

A painter is not a picture, and he does not die if his picture is destroyed. You may say, "He's put a lot of himself into it," but you only mean that all its beauty and interest has come out of his head. His skill is not in the picture in the same way that it is in his head, or even in his hands. I expect you see how this difference between Pantheists and Christians hangs together with the other one. If you do not take the distinction between good and bad very seriously, then it is easy to say that anything you find in this world is a part of God. But, of course, if you think some things really bad, and God really good, then you cannot talk like that.

You must believe that God is separate from the world and that some of the things we see in it are contrary to His will. Confronted with a cancer or a slum the Pantheist can say, "If you could only see it from the divine point of view, you would realize that this also is God." The Christian replies, "Don't talk damned nonsense." (*)

[*] One listener complained of the word damned as frivolous swearing. But I mean exactly what I say—nonsense that is damned is under God's curse, and will (apart from God's grace) lead those who believe it to eternal death.

For Christianity is a fighting religion. It thinks God made the world—that space and time, heat and cold, and all the colors and tastes, and all the animals and vegetables, are things that God "made up out of His head" as a man makes up a story. But it also thinks that a great many things have gone wrong with the world that God made and that God insists, and insists very loudly, on our putting them right again.

NOTES

 ©2010, 2017. Wheaton Press™ All Rights Reserved.

Mere Christianity, Book 2

"By the humility and gentleness of Christ, I appeal to you—I, Paul, who am 'timid' when face to face with you, but "bold" toward you when away! I beg you that when I come may not have to be as bold as I expect to be toward some people who think that we live by the standards of this world. For though we live in the world, we do not wage war as the world does. The weapons we fight with are not the weapons of the world. On the contrary, they have divine power to demolish strongholds. We demolish arguments and every pretension that sets itself up against the knowledge of God, and we take captive every thought to make it obedient to Christ."

2 Corinthians 10:1-5 (NIV)

3. ATHIESM & MEANINGLESSNESS (P38 & 39)

"That raises a very big question. If a good God made the world why has it gone wrong? And for many years I simply refused to listen to the Christian answers to this question, because I kept on feeling "whatever you say, and however clever your arguments are, isn't it much simpler and easier to say that the world was not made by any intelligent power? Aren't all your arguments simply a complicated attempt to avoid the obvious?" But then that threw me back into another difficulty.

My argument against God was that the universe seemed so cruel and unjust. But how had I got this idea of just and unjust? A man does not call a line crooked unless he has some idea of a straight line. What was I comparing this universe with when I called it unjust? If the whole show was bad and senseless from A to Z, so to speak, why did I, who was supposed to be part of the show, find myself in such violent reaction against it? A man feels wet when he falls into water, because man is not a water animal: a fish would not feel wet.

Of course I could have given up my idea of justice by saying it was nothing but a private idea of my own. But if I did that, then my argument against God collapsed too— for the argument depended on saying that the world was really unjust, not simply that it did not happen to please my private fancies. Thus in the very act of trying to prove that God did not exist—in other words, that the whole of reality was senseless—I found I was forced to assume that one part of reality—namely my idea of justice—was full of sense.
Consequently atheism turns out to be too simple. If the whole universe has no meaning, we should never have found out that it has no meaning: just as, if there were no light in the universe and therefore no creatures with eyes, we should never know it was dark. Dark would be without meaning.

NOTES:

©2010, 2017. Wheaton Press™ All Rights Reserved.

Mere Christianity, Book 2

"By the humility and gentleness of Christ, I appeal to you—I, Paul, who am 'timid' when face to face with you, but "bold" toward you when away! I beg you that when I come may not have to be as bold as I expect to be toward some people who think that we live by the standards of this world. For though we live in the world, we do not wage war as the world does. The weapons we fight with are not the weapons of the world. On the contrary, they have divine power to demolish strongholds. We demolish arguments and every pretension that sets itself up against the knowledge of God, and we take captive every thought to make it obedient to Christ."

2 Corinthians 10:1-5 (NIV)

4. "All sin is spoiled goodness" (pg. 44, 48)

If Dualism is true, then the bad Power must be a being who likes badness for its own sake. But in reality we have no experience of anyone liking badness just because it is bad. The nearest we can get to it is in cruelty. But in real life people are cruel for one of two reasons- either because they are sadists, that is, because they have a sexual perversion which makes cruelty a cause of sensual pleasure to them, or else for the sake of something they are going to get out of it-money, or power, or safety. But pleasure, money, power, and safety are all, as far as they go, good things. The badness consists in pursuing them by the wrong method, or in the wrong way, or too much. I do not mean, of course, that the people who do this are not desperately wicked. I do mean that wickedness, when you examine it, turns out to be the pursuit of some good in the wrong way. You can be good for the mere sake of goodness: you cannot be bad for the mere sake of badness. You can do a kind action when you are not feeling kind and when it gives you no pleasure, simply because kindness is right; but no one ever did a cruel action simply because cruelty is wrong-only because cruelty was pleasant or useful to him. In other words badness cannot succeed even in being bad in the same way in which goodness is good. Goodness is, so to speak, itself: badness is only spoiled goodness. And there must be something good first before it can be spoiled. We called sadism a sexual perversion; but you must first have the idea of a normal sexuality before you can talk of its being perverted; and you can see which is the perversion, because you can explain the perverted from the normal, and cannot explain the normal from the perverted. It follows that this Bad Power, who is supposed to be on an equal footing with the Good Power, and to love badness in the same way as the Good Power loves goodness, is a mere bogy. In order to be bad he must have good things to want and then to pursue in the wrong way: he must have impulses which were originally good in order to be able to pervert them. But if he is bad he cannot supply himself either with good things to desire or with good impulses to pervert. He must be getting both from the Good Power. And if so, then he is not independent. He is part of the Good Power's world: he was made either by the Good Power or by some power above them both.

Put it more simply still. To be bad, he must exist and have intelligence and will. But existence, intelligence and will are in themselves good. Therefore he must be getting them from the Good Power: even to be bad he must borrow or steal from his opponent. And do you now begin to see why Christianity has always said that the devil is a fallen angel? That is not a mere story for the children. It is a real recognition of the fact that evil is a parasite, not an original thing. The powers which enable evil to carry on are powers given it by goodness. All the things which enable a bad man to be effectively bad are in themselves good things-resolution, cleverness, good looks, existence itself. That is why Dualism, in a strict sense, will not work.

NOTES:

 ©2010, 2017. Wheaton Press™ All Rights Reserved.

Mere Christianity, Book 2

"By the humility and gentleness of Christ, I appeal to you—I, Paul, who am 'timid' when face to face with you, but "bold" toward you when away! I beg you that when I come may not have to be as bold as I expect to be toward some people who think that we live by the standards of this world. For though we live in the world, we do not wage war as the world does. The weapons we fight with are not the weapons of the world. On the contrary, they have divine power to demolish strongholds. We demolish arguments and every pretension that sets itself up against the knowledge of God, and we take captive every thought to make it obedient to Christ."

2 Corinthians 10:1-5 (NIV)

5. Layers of free will: a free will parfait (pg. 47-48)

Christians, then, believe that an evil power has made himself for the present the Prince of this World. And, of course, that raises problems. Is this state of affairs in accordance with God's will or not? If it is, He is a strange God, you will say: and if it is not, how can anything happen contrary to the will of a being with absolute power?

But anyone who has been in authority knows how a thing can be in accordance with your will in one way and not in another. It may be quite sensible for a mother to say to the children, "I'm not going to go and make you tidy the schoolroom every night. You've got to learn to keep it tidy on your own." Then she goes up one night and finds the Teddy bear and the ink and the French Grammar all lying in the grate. That is against her will. She would prefer the children to be tidy. But on the other hand, it is her will which has left the children free to be untidy. The same thing arises in any regiment, or trade union, or school. You make a thing voluntary and then half the people do not do it. That is not what you willed, but your will has made it possible.

It is probably the same in the universe. God created things which had free will. That means creatures which can go either wrong or right. Some people think they can imagine a creature which was free but had no possibility of going wrong; I cannot. If a thing is free to be good it is also free to be bad. And free will is what has made evil possible. Why, then, did God give them free will? Because free will though it makes evil possible, is also the only thing that makes possible any love or goodness or joy worth having. A world of automata-of creatures that worked like machines-would hardly be worth creating. The happiness which God designs for His higher creatures is the happiness of being freely, voluntarily united to Him and to each other in an ecstasy of love and delight compared with which the most rapturous love between a man and a woman on this earth is mere milk and water. And for that they must be free.
*Of course God knew what would happen if they used their freedom the wrong way: **apparently He thought it worth the risk**. Perhaps we feel inclined to disagree with Him. But there is a difficulty about disagreeing with God. He is the source from which all your reasoning power comes: you could not be right and He wrong any more than a stream can rise higher than its own source. When you are arguing against Him you are arguing against the very power that makes you able to argue at all: it is like cutting off the branch you are sitting on. If God thinks this state of war in the universe a price worth paying for free will-that is, for making a live world in which creatures can do real good or harm and something of real importance can happen, instead of a toy world which only moves when He pulls the strings-then we may take it it is worth paying.*

- Layer #1:

- Layer #2:

- Layer #3:

- Layer #4:

➤ Worth the Risk? *(The high school banquet story)*

©2010, 2017. Wheaton Press™ All Rights Reserved.

Mere Christianity, Book 2

6. Lord, Liar, Lunatic (pg. 52)

I am trying here to prevent anyone saying the really foolish thing that people often say about Him: "I'm ready to accept Jesus as a great moral teacher, but I don't accept His claim to be God." That is the one thing we must not say. A man who was merely a man and said the sort of things Jesus said would not be a great moral teacher. He would either be a lunatic-on a level with the man who says he is a poached egg-or else he would be the Devil of Hell. You must make your choice. Either this man was, and is, the Son of God: or else a madman or something worse. You can shut Him up for a fool, you can spit at Him and kill Him as a demon; or you can fall at His feet and call Him Lord and God. But let us not come with any patronizing nonsense about His being a great human teacher. He has not left that open to us. He did not intend to.

NOTES:

7. How it works (pg. 55, 64)

On my view the theories are not themselves the thing you are asked to accept. Many of you no doubt have read Jeans or Eddington. What they do when they want to explain the atom, or something of that sort, is to give you a description out of which you can make a mental picture. But then they warn you that this picture is not what the scientists actually believe. What the scientists believe is a mathematical formula. The pictures are there only to help you to understand the formula. They are not really true in the way the formula is; they do not give you the real thing but only something more or less like it. They are only meant to help, and if they do not help you can drop them. The thing itself cannot be pictured, it can only be expressed mathematically. We are in the same boat here. We believe that the death of Christ is just that point in history at which something absolutely unimaginable from outside shows through into our own world. And if we cannot picture even the atoms of which our own world is built, of course we are not going to be able to picture this. Indeed, if we found that we could fully understand it, that very fact would show it was not what it professes to be-the inconceivable, the uncreated, the thing from beyond nature, striking down into nature like lightning. You may ask what good will it be to us if we do not understand it. But that is easily answered. A man can eat his dinner without understanding exactly how food nourishes him. **A man can accept what Christ has done without knowing how it works: indeed, he certainly would not know how it works until he has accepted it.**

We are told that Christ was killed for us, that His death has washed out our sins, and that by dying He disabled death itself. That is the formula. That is Christianity. That is what has to be believed. Any theories we build up as to how Christ's death did all this are, in my view, quite secondary: mere plans or diagrams to be left alone if they do not help us, and, even if they do help us, not to be confused with the thing itself. All the same, some of these theories are worth looking at.

NOTES:

8. Why Jesus? (pg. 57)

The one most people have heard is the one I mentioned before -the one about our being let off because Christ had volunteered to bear a punishment instead of us. Now on the face of it that is a very silly theory. If God was prepared to let us off, why on earth did He not do so? And what possible point could there be in punishing an innocent person instead? None at all that I can see, if you are thinking of punishment in the police-court sense. On the other hand, if you think of a debt, there is plenty of point in a person who has some assets paying it on behalf of someone who has not. Or if you take "paying the penalty," not in the sense of being punished, but in the more general sense of "standing the racket" or "footing the bill," then, of course, it is a matter of common experience that, when one person has got himself into a hole, the trouble of getting him out usually falls on a kind friend. Now what was the sort of "hole" man had got himself into? He had tried to set up on his own, to behave as if he belonged to himself. In other words, fallen man is not simply an imperfect creature who needs improvement: he is a rebel who must lay down his arms. Laying down your arms, surrendering, saying you are sorry, realizing that you have been on the wrong track and getting ready to start life over again from the ground floor-that is the only way out of a "hole." This process of surrender-this movement full speed astern-is what Christians call repentance. Now repentance is no fun at all. It is something much harder than merely eating humble pie. It means unlearning all the self-conceit and self-will that we have been training ourselves into for thousands of years. It means killing part of yourself, undergoing a kind of death. In fact, it needs a good man to repent. And here comes the catch. Only a bad person needs to repent: only a good person can repent perfectly. The worse you are the more you need it and the less you can do it. The only person who could do it perfectly would be a perfect person-and he would not need it.

NOTES:

      ©2010, 2017. Wheaton Press™ All Rights Reserved.

Scripture Reading Integrity Assignments
Romans and *Mere Christianity*, Book 1 & 2

Read and annotate the letter to the church at Rome written by the Apostle Paul as a letter in one sitting. Pretend you are a member of the church. Where do you see connections to our discussion on Lewis's argument for the existence of God in the opening 30 pages of *Mere Christianity?* The connections you make can be subtle, overt, literary, historical, artistic, personal, or metaphoric.

In the space below, write at least three verses that you find engaging, and briefly explain why you picked these verses. Cut and paste or write out the entire verse, but do not simply put the reference. Do not summarize the verse as a response.

©2010, 2017. Wheaton Press™ All Rights Reserved.

The Parable of Grace

Compare and Contrast Idealism and Christ Centered Theism

This is the Fellowship of the Rings' test " and the "Book of Acts test" - "EMAIL HOME" that was emailed students' families for 15 years to help compare and contrast Idealism with Gospel Centered Authentic Christianity and to make families aware and invite the families in on the discussion.

"Dear Parents and Guardians of current "Inklings" Students

Let me start by saying that I love my job and your students; we have been having a great time exploring the nature of reality, C. S. Lewis's Mere Christianity, and Chesterton's Orthodoxy. I am sad to see this semester come to a close; but I am excited to see what your students do with our final exam on spiritual formation, authentic discipleship, and journey.

I want to share with you a practical learning opportunity that I put into action a few weeks ago as we were setting up the more detailed theological study of Christian Theism. I have found it to be fruitful to help students get a firm grasp on the actual nature of True Biblical Grace by not simply talking about it in class, but by walking through it in an authentic way. While this lesson has inherent risks, particularly the potential abuse of grace and the misuse of the parable format, I allow the students to EXPERIENCE real grace in the language of education and the context of real Idealism. The lesson is experiential in nature and has been approved and blessed by the administration. I have been doing this lesson for over 15 years and have found that it can be powerful and life transformative for many students who are willing to take it to heart. This email is an attempt to connect you with the information in case of questions that might arise, grade issues, and concerns that may develop in communication.

Furthermore, as a follow up to the lesson I want to encourage you to ask your student about the experience and to engage in a conversation about this topic. It was a two-week lesson and the class just took their Test on the Book of Acts. The "Essential Study Guide" for the Book of acts Test is attached BELOW. Please carefully read it before you talk to you student or me. Some of you may recognize this lesson; I used to use The Fellowship of The Rings for the test.

Here are three key things that help make this lesson profoundly poignant:
1) It is essential that you respect your student's dignity and free will in the process. Each student had to freely accept or reject the grace on his or her own terms. In short – students were not pressured, nor should they have been pressured, either way. This should and will make for some great discussion and testimony time… but please be a resource and mentor not an "authority figure" in this process. Fear is not our friend when it comes to grace. (The truth is, that over 1,000 students have experienced this lesson - only one has refused the grace.)
2) Please keep in mind that this is a real experiential lesson and not a "simulation." Again, be sure to read the "Essential Study Guide" BELOW.
3) This lesson isolates the truth and nature of authentic grace. It is not about our responsibility to willingly dedicate our lives as living sacrifices of praise, nor is it focused on the good works planned for each of us from before we were born! These other truths are why we end the class with Narnia, Hobbit, and Lord of the Rings - with Journey and Adventure as authentic Disciples of Christ. I am fully aware that we all need to get out of our "Hobbit Holes" and "slay dragons" and "destroy evil rings" all the while empowered buy God's Holy Spirit with our unique gifting and calling and our "Fellowship" of believers...

Thanks again for ALL that you do to encourage your students; we are having a great time learning and growing together this semester. I am excited to share this lesson in such close proximity to Christmas and for the first time with the Book of Acts! I know this is a long email at a busy time of year, thanks for taking the time to read it and thanks for all of your support and prayers.

Peace, Hope, Joy to you.
Matthew Dominguez

 ©2010, 2017. Wheaton Press™ All Rights Reserved.

The Parable of Grace

Compare and Contrast Idealism and Christ Centered Theism

This is the unique Fellowship of the Rings' test " and the "Book of Acts test" ESSENTIAL Study Guide" That was used with students for 15 years to help compare and contrast Idealism with Gospel Centered Authentic Christianity.

AKA: Parable of Grace

Dearest Philosophy students,

I am so glad that you took the time and effort to find this "study guide". Welcome to another adventure in learning! I do want to remind you that the main goal of my class is to learn; and if you have not noticed yet, learning often comes in a variety of packages. This lesson is packaged in the intricate yet familiar structure of a parable.

We are going to use the traditional evaluation tool of the classic "100 point Test" to help learn more about the 4 different philosophies and salvation through Grace. And yes, we will also simultaneously be evaluating your understanding of Fellowship of the Ring. We will definitely discuss all of this in more detail in class (and at other times if you wish) but for this part of the lesson here is the essential information you will need to pass this test.

I know that this test will be nearly impossible for you to pass on your own; please remember that in class I announced that this is a pass/fail test. To pass you need a perfect score. Without a perfect score you fail, which for this test equals a ZERO. (BTW: Due to the nature of Idealism, as shadows your grade is actually already a Zero…) I want to clarify that I am intentionally designing a few of the questions on this test so that Tolkien himself might have a hard time getting a perfect score. For example, since the evaluation is about the book Fellowship of the Ring, or the Book of Acts, I can ask ANYTHING from the book on the test. Basically, by implication, unless you have memorized the text in the next two weeks, you would not be able to answer this type of question: "What is the 5th word on the 10th line on such and such a page" or "what is the exact wording of such and such a verse in the tenth chapter." Notice how this type of evaluation fits with an Idealist's or even Religious Christian Theistic philosophy, which demands absolute perfection.

The "ONE WAY" that you can ENSURE that you will pass this test is to trust your teacher to provide another way, which he has. You will receive a perfect score on this test by asking for one and believing in your heart that you will receive one. Please note: your performance on the test, which you will still take, has no effect on your score of 100%; unless of course you choose to not have a 100% going into the test and try to actually achieve this perfect score through your own diligence and hard work. Be aware that the choice is yours; You have a zero on the test right now, you may choose to ask and receive a perfect score before you take the test, or you may choose to accept your current Zero for now and strive for a perfect score on your own through taking the test and accepting the score your get. Remember, you could simply believe that Mr. D. will do what he says, and your could ask for a Perfect Grade from your teacher, and thus receive your Perfect Score in advance as a free gift.

Please Note: This perfect score will be irrevocably granted to all who believe that I will do this and ask me to do it BEFORE the test is taken. You will receive the perfect score on Academy Central as soon as you believe and ask. Nothing you do or say will take the grade off of Academy Central, unless you personally choose for me to take it off and ask me to do so in person and in writing. As you prepare for your test, that your are still taking, enjoy the FREEDOM and PEACE that comes with REAL GRACE.

I hope to see or hear from you all soon. I love having you in class; it is a joy and honor to learn and grow with you. Embrace the grace.

With Joy and Love,

Mr. Dominguez

P.S. I hope and trust that this is "good news" for you. You ARE encouraged to share this news with your fellow classmates.

P.P.S. You will be asked to formally comment on our class discussion blog on academy central after the test; feel free to comment initially and spontaneously before you are required to do so, it will be great to get the dialogue going…

"For it is by Grace you have been saved, through faith – and this not from yourselves, it is the gift of God – not by works, so that no man one can boast" Ephesians 2: 8-9

"If you confess with your mouth 'Jesus is Lord,' and believe in your heart that God raised him from the dead, you will be saved. For it is with your heart that you believe and are Justified, and it is with your mouth that you confess and are saved." Romans 10: 9-10

"For god so loved the world that He gave his one and only Son, that whoever believes in Him shall not perish but have eternal life." John 3:16

"Don't be afraid," the prophet answered. "Those who are with us are more than those who are with them." And Elisha prayed, "O Lord, open his eyes so he may see." II Kings 6:16&17

The Parable of Grace

Compare and Contrast: Idealism and Authentic Gospel Centered Christianity

Class Discussion Notes:

"Even
After
All this time
The Sun never says to the Earth,

'You owe me.'

Look
What happens
With a love like that,
It lights the whole sky."

— حافظ

Reflection: Rewrite the parable of grace in your own words as though you are telling a roommate in college about this assignment, recalling the good old days of Inklings, philosophy, theology, and worldview.

 ©2010, 2017. Wheaton Press™ All Rights Reserved.

The Midterm Project
Culminating Creative, Summative Assessment Assignment
Philosophy, the Nature of Reality, Chesterton, and *Mere Christianity*

Assignment Options:

1. **LETTER:** You can write a letter to C.S. Lewis or G.K. Chesterton that incorporates a description of your spiritual journey synthesized with our philosophical studies of the nature of reality, *Orthodoxy*, and *Mere Christianity*. The language you choose for the letter should be respectful and academic. The context of your conversation is this semester here and now; you are to pretend that the Inklings group is alive and well. The genres you may choose from include a very personal letter or a formal letter to a professor. Please note: you are also expected to write a brief explanatory introduction explaining your intent and setting.

Expectations:
   1) At least three quotes from *Mere Christianity*. Provide page numbers.
   2) Provide a brief explanatory introduction at the beginning of the paper
   3) Word minimum: 800 words including introduction
   4) Be creative and insightful. Show interpretive understanding of the content of Lewis's passages and our philosophical studies and discussions on the nature of the reality. This means that you are not simply copying Chesterton or Lewis's words onto your paper.
   5) Turn the paper in typed
   6) Turn the paper in on time: Due on or before: _____

2. **DIALOGUE:** You may choose to create a dialogue. Be sure to clearly explain the overarching context of the conversation, the basic worldviews and personalities of the characters, and the immediate characteristics of the setting and issue/issues. The dialogue should be between at least three characters representing three philosophies, with Lewis or Chesterton as one of the characters who represents the Christian theistic philosophy. Remember, we have discussed the power of language and the potential of conversation. Work hard to make the conversation meaningful, and be sure to have a beginning, middle, and conclusion. It will help to pick an issue or two to discuss in the assignment or to address a few of the philosophy questions from your notes. Be sure to include an explanatory introduction and cite your quotes on a works cited page.

Expectations:
   1) At least three quotes from *Mere Christianity*. Give page numbers.
   2) Provide a brief explanatory introduction at the beginning of the paper (the setting, vision, and interpretation explanation as well as the characters and authors along with their basic worldview).
   3) Word minimum: 800 words including introduction
   4) Be creative and insightful. Show interpretive understanding of the content of Lewis's passages and our philosophical studies and discussions on the nature of the reality. This means that you are not simply copying Chesterton or Lewis's words onto your paper.
   5) Turn the paper in typed
   6) Turn the paper in on time: Due on or before: _____

3. **COLLAGE-SCRAPBOOK:** You can create a quotations and images collage or scrapbook for philosophy, Chesterton, and *Mere Christianity*. The goal of this assignment is to creatively incorporate images, photographs, artwork, etc. that represent selected quotes and passages in order to express a theme or interconnected themes from what we have been studying. You need to use at least 10 quotes from *Mere Christianity* or *Orthodoxy* specifically synthesized with 10 quotes on philosophy and the nature of reality from other sources, and at least 7 images. Be sure to include a 2-3 paragraph explanatory introduction and cite your quotes on a works cited page.

Expectations:
   1) At least 20 total quotes: 10 from *Mere Christianity* or *Orthodoxy* and 10 philosophy/reality quotes. Be sure to cite your sources using page numbers and website domains.
   2) At least 7 images (cite your sources).
   3) Brief explanatory introduction (2-3 paragraphs). Put on the back of the collage. This should be the setting and/or vision and interpretation explanation. This should include your main theme of the collage.
   4) Be creative and insightful. Show interpretive understanding of the content of Lewis's passages and our nature of reality discussions. This means you are not simply copying Lewis's words onto your paper.
   5) Have it all typed (see "Typed Writing Assignments" handout) including quotes for collages unless you have special artistic permission.
   6) Hand it in on time. Due on or before: _____

4. **CELEBRATION OF GIFTS CREATIVE PROJECT:** You may also do an alternative creative project. Please keep in mind the requirements below as you determine what to do. You will need to approve your idea via a detailed, typed proposal of your plan. You must type out your proposal in complete sentences and explain in detail what you plan on doing, how you plan to do it, and how you plan on incorporating your work into the expectations listed below. Your teacher will approve well-developed and clearly planned projects. Note: If you plan on being in a group, please explain how each group member will be clearly and concretely contribute to the project in your proposal.

Expectations:
   1) A typed proposal approved by your teacher
   2) Brief explanatory four paragraph summary of the project placed at the beginning of the paper, on the back of the collages, or alongside your project. Explain the setting and/or vision, main theme, and an interpretation explanation of your project.
   3) Be creative and insightful. Show interpretive understanding of the content of Lewis's passages and class discussions on the nature of reality. This means that you are not simply copying Lewis's or Chesterton's words onto your paper.
   4) Have the written component typed (see "Typed Writing Assignments" handout)
   5) Hand it in on time. Due on or before: _____

Be creative and try to enjoy this assignment. Please help each other dialogically with this project; however, keep in mind that each student is expected to turn in his or her own project. Please note that there is not an option for group written papers or collages unless you creatively propose a clever option for #4.

MIDTERM Self Assessment: Creative, Summative Assessment Assignment
Self-evaluation and grading sheet for **#4 CELEBRATION OF GIFTS** midterm project

Name: _____ Period: _____ Project:

"Each one should use whatever gift he (or she) has received to serve others, faithfully, administering God's grace in various forms." (1 Peter 4:10)

"We have different gifts according to the grace given us." (Romans 12:6)

"There are different kinds of gifts, but the same Spirit. There are different kinds of service, but the same Lord. There are different kinds of working, but the same God works all of them in all people." (1 Corinthians 12:4)

My basic objective for this project is to utilize my giftedness to create something original and unique that has to do with my study of philosophy, Chesterton, and *Mere Christianity*. The project is open-ended and limited only by my creativity and a few guidelines.

The Requirements:

1) Did I approve my idea with my teacher on time?

    Yes   No   Other   Comments:

2) Is the project original (new/different) and unique?

    Yes   No   Other   Comments:

3) Does the project display effort, creativity, and thoughtfulness?

    Yes   No   Other   Comments:

4) Does the project reflect synthesized learning of principles, concepts, lessons, truths, virtues, and/or general aspects of philosophy and *Mere Christianity* that we studied this semester?

    Yes   No   Other   Comments:

5) Did I put in the appropriate time in developing and creating my project (2-4 hours)? If I worked on this project for much more than the allotted time, did I get permission to do so?

    Hours Spent: Yes   No   Other   Comments:

6) Did I hand in a four-paragraph typed explanation of my project?
    a) "Explain why I chose this project and what I have learned through creating this project."
    b) "Explain what I have synthesized and how - & the Sources you used!"
    c) "Explain what my project means and why what I did is significant to our study of Philosophy and "Mere Christianity.""
    d) "Provide a brief justification of the time and effort spent on the project."

    Yes   No   Other   Comments:

7) The completed project was due on _____. Were the project and presentation turned in on time? If appropriate: Did I explain and/or present my project to the class?

    Yes   No   Other   Comments:

My grade will reflect how fully and appropriately I have met all seven of the requirements listed above. My grade for the "Celebration of Gifts Assessment" is worth 100 points total.

Grade: _____ / 100

Additional comments on the project and/or your project grade:

©2010, 2017. Wheaton Press™ All Rights Reserved.

©2010, 2017. Wheaton Press™ All Rights Reserved.

Unit 4
(ACT 4)

"The Word Became Flesh":
AN INCARNATIONAL
View of the World

Philosophy & Theology

INVITED TO TRUST

UNIT 4 (Act 4) ESSENTIAL QUESTIONS:

1. What is *an Incarnational world view?*
2. *What does it mean to get beyond philosophy, religion, and stories into an Authentic Relationship with God?*
3. What does it mean to have an "Encounter with the Living God"?
4. What Is an Aslan Moment?
5. Why is Jesus essential to an authentic Incarnational World View?
6. How can I use Lewis's Book , The Great Divorce to understand My invitation to Kingdom Living "Here and Now"
7. How can I use Lewis's Book , The Last Battle top understand False Versions of Christ in our modern culture and religions?
8. Why is a true encounter and authentic relationship with the Living God of Love so Powerful?

UNIT 4 (Act 4) READINGS:

1. Lewis, C.S. *The Great Divorce*
2. *James*
3. Lewis, C.S. *The Last Battle*
4. *Galatians*

UNIT 4 (Act 4) THINKBOOK LEARNING OPPORTUNITIES:

Formative:
- ❏ *The Great Divorce* Quiz and Notes (Preface, Chapters 1-3)
- ❏ *The Great Divorce* Character Profile for a Shadowy Character
- ❏ *The Great Divorce* Character Profile for a Solid Person
- ❏ Scripture Reading "Truth Revealed": *James* and *The Great Divorce*
- ❏ Scripture Reading "Truth Revealed": *Galatians and The Last Battle*
- ❏ Personal Refection on the "Aslan Moment & an Encounter with the Living God"

UNIT 4 (Act 4) LEARNING PLAN:

1. This is not a Pipe
2. *What is an authentic Encounter and Relationship with the Living God?*
2. *How to read The Great Divorce…*
3. *The Great Divorce*
4. *James*
5. The Last Battle
6. Galatians
7. *The "Aslan Moment"*

"This Is Not a Pipe"
Quotes, notes, doodles, and discussion

Photo Magritte "Treachery of Images" public domain

We are told that Christ was killed for us, that His death has washed out our sins, and that by dying He disabled death itself. That is the formula. That is Christianity. That is what has to be believed. Any theories we build up as to how Christ's death did all this are, in my view, quite secondary: mere plans or diagrams to be left alone if they do not help us, and, even if they do help us, not to be confused with the thing itself. All the same, some of these theories are worth looking at.

C.S. Lewis Mere Christianity Page 56

A map is not the territory it represents,
but, if correct, it has a similar structure to the territory, which accounts for its usefulness.
— Alfred Korzybski, Science and Sanity (1933, p. 58)

©2010, 2017. Wheaton Press™ All Rights Reserved.

"The Hug"

Pilot asks "What is truth?" in John 18:38. It is standing right in front of him. The roman quest for truth was an abstract concept, or a set of ideas, or the right string of words.

However, The Truth is a Being, The Being, The Living God. John Says the "Logos" became Flesh...The truth is incarnational: "in–carne" – in the flesh. The Truth is The Person right in front of Pilot. In John 14:6 Jesus says "I am the the way the TRUTH the Life…"

In John 20:16-18 Mary has a powerful encounter with Jesus. She actually gets the first Hug from the risen savior – she literally hugs the TRUTH – and then becomes the first evangelist!

This is the concept of "Perichoresis" embodied in Jesus. The Trinity is perpetually inviting all of us, the Beloved, into the Divine Dance of His Love.

Artwork public domain

What does it mean to have an authentic encounter and relationship with the Living Loving God of the universe?

How does this connect with the lessons on Perichoresis?

Describe the personal unique touch in the following Jesus Encounter Moments in the Bible. How does the concept of Perichoresis fit these passages?:

- A Conversation with the woman at the well in John 4:
- Dignity for the woman caught in adultery in John 8:
- A Conversation with Nicodemus in John 3:
- Dinner with Zacchaeus in Luke 19:
- Personal touch with Malcus and his ear in John 18:
- Peter's numerous Encounters (google them…):
- John resting his head on the shoulder of the Truth at Dinner in John 13:
- Thomas and Jesus in John 20:
- The Walk with Jesus to Emmaus in Luke 24:
- Pentecost! In the opening chapters of the Book of Acts:
- Philip and the Ethiopian's Encounter in Acts 8:
- Paul's Divine Encounter on the The Road to Damascus in Acts 9!

 ©2010, 2017. Wheaton Press™ All Rights Reserved.

Brave New World of Philosophy: The Fullness of Reality
A New Way of Seeing

What Is "Perichoresis"

"Perichoresis" – The Dance of Love!

The theologians in the early church tried to describe this wonderful reality that we call Trinity. If any of you have ever been to a Greek wedding, you may have seen their distinctive way of dancing . . . It's called perichoresis. There are not two dancers, but at least three. They start to go in circles, weaving in and out in this very beautiful pattern of motion. They start to go faster and faster and faster, all the while staying in perfect rhythm and in sync with each other. Eventually, they are dancing so quickly (yet so effortlessly) that as you look at them, it just becomes a blur. Their individual identities are part of a larger dance. The early church fathers and mothers looked at that dance (perichoresis) and said, "That's what the Trinity is like." It's a harmonious set of relationship in which there is mutual giving and receiving. This relationship is called love, and it's what the Trinity is all about. The Perichoresis is the dance of love.
–Jonathan Marlow

John 17:20-22
20 "I am praying not only for these disciples but also for all who will ever believe in me through their message. 21 I pray that they will all be one, just as you and I are one—as you are in me, Father, and I am in you. And may they be in us so that the world will believe you sent me. 22 "I have given them the glory you gave me, so they may be one as we are one.

The Lord of the Dance

Watch and Listen to the Lord of the Dance Song!
Feel free to look up the version by Sydney Carter.

Lord of the Dance lyrics and music are copyright by Sydney Carter the song itself is famous worldwide particularly through Riverdance.

As Kingfishers Catch Fire
BY GERARD MANLEY HOPKINS

As kingfishers catch fire, dragonflies draw flame;
As tumbled over rim in roundy wells
Stones ring; like each tucked string tells, each hung bell's
Bow swung finds tongue to fling out broad its name;
Each mortal thing does one thing and the same:
Deals out that being indoors each one dwells;
Selves — goes itself; myself it speaks and spells,
Crying Whát I dó is me: for that I came.

I say móre: the just man justices;
Keeps grace: thát keeps all his goings graces;
Acts in God's eye what in God's eye he is —
Chríst — for Christ plays in ten thousand places,
Lovely in limbs, and lovely in eyes not his
To the Father through the features of men's faces.

©2010, 2017. Wheaton Press™ All Rights Reserved.

Brave New World of Philosophy: The Fullness of Reality
A New Way of Seeing

"To them God has chosen to make known among the Gentiles the glorious riches of this mystery, which is Christ in you, the hope of glory". Colossians 1:27

This diagram describes all four circles intermingling and balancing one another – this is the expression of a complete, balanced truth.. This Truth is best explained through the Person of Jesus Christ, as in Him, all four worldviews are expressed perfectly, together in unity , without extreme. And in loving relationship; with people.

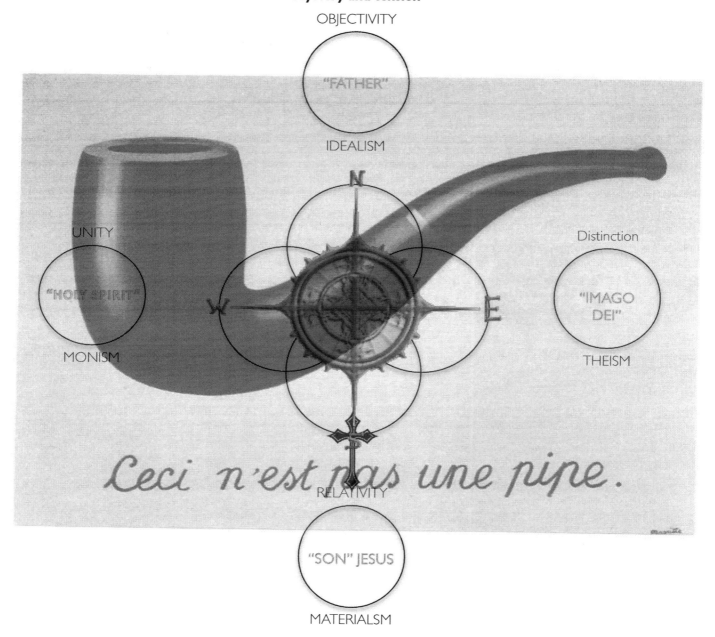

Grace and truth
Paradox and oxymoron
Mystery and tension

OBJECTIVITY

"FATHER"

IDEALISM

UNITY

"HOLY SPIRIT"

MONISM

Distinction

"IMAGO DEI"

THEISM

RELATIVITY

Ceci n'est pas une pipe.

"SON" JESUS

MATERIALSM

 ©2010, 2017. Wheaton Press™ All Rights Reserved.

The Great Divorce: An Invitation to Joy
Quotes, notes, doodles, and discussion

Photo public domain

Artwork courtesy of Princess Allison Spoelhof

Door #1: "Heaven and Hell" The Kingdom is Real! (Key theme: People Choose Hell.)

Door #2: "Earth" Thy Kingdom Come…" (Key theme: Evangelism is a perpetual invitation to Joy!)

Door #3: "The Landscape of your Soul" The Kingdom of god is within you…" (Key theme: Transformation from your dead self, the false self, into your new alive self, the true self.)

©2010, 2017. Wheaton Press™ All Rights Reserved.

Philosophy & Theology

The Great Divorce: Character grid by chapter

Ch.	Shadow Character	Key Issue, Struggle, or Sin	Shadow's Choice	Solid Character
1	The "Queue"	Choosing to get in line or stay in line		
2	Those on the Bus	Warped perspective of Christ's Kingdom: Selfish Ignorance – "Fixed Faces full not possibility, but impossibility."	To check things out	Jesus, the ultimate Bus Driver
3	"Man-shaped Stains on the Air"	When have we got to go back?	Grey Town	
4	The Mean, Demanding Boss	Warped view of Independence and Misuse of Freedom and Power: Wants His "Rights"; will not ask for help.	Grey Town	Len, a Forgiven Murderer & A Saint
5	The Apostate Egotistical Theologian	Warped Theology: Does not believe that Jesus needed to die for his sins. Does not believe in his need for "crude" salvation.	Grey Town	Dick, the "Simple Minded" Theologian and Friend
6	"Ikey," the shadow with the Bowler Hat	Warped use of Christ's Riches and Gifts; Lack of trust in God to Provide: Greed. He wants to exploit the solid country for his own gain in the shadowy world. He wants to use the things of Christ's Kingdom to further his own shadowy kingdom	Grey Town	A Bright Angel who stood "like one Crucified" in the massive waterfall
7	Hard-Bitten shadow	Warped use of Trust: Mistrust and Sinicism. Thinks everybody should entertain him. Will not take responsibility.	Grey Town	None—he would not trust or listen to anyone at all
8	Girl filled with Shame	Warped Identity & Humility and Warped use of Appearance: Filled with such shame that she focuses only on self. Her identity is in her image and her shame instead of who she is in Christ.	Grey Town? (Not sure)	Confident, Fiery Angel (the Solid One)
9	The Narrator The Grumbling Grandma The Artist	Warped use of time: Indecision, focused on others and not enough on self. Lack of will. Warped Attitude and Warped use of Suffering: Hyper-Focused on negative circumstances, complainer; not focused on Christ and his power. Warped use of Talents: Using art to form and sustain his identity verses painting from his identity in Christ and Painting for Christ.	Not sure Grey Town Grey Town	- George MacDonald - Bright Patience at her side - Joy-filled Artist
10	The Controlling Wife (Robert's wife)	Warped Marital LOVE: Finding value, power, and identity in controlling others not in Christ. Needs to submit to Christ's Authority.	Grey Town	Hilda
11	Pam, the Obsessive Mom Man with the Lizard on his shoulder	Warped Maternal LOVE: Used her role as mom and her son for her identity and to fill her own personal needs rather than Christ. Warped Sexual Intimacy & LOVE: Lust – sexual impurity – impure thoughts and deeds	Grey Town Solid Country	- Pam's Brother - White-hot Flaming Spirit of Purity
12 & 13	Sarah Smith's Husband and The Tragedian	Warped Romantic LOVE: Codependency and selfish manipulation of people's compassion and pity using exaggeration and lying: acting.	Grey Town	Sarah Smith: Free, Joy-filled, and Genuine Love
14	The narrator	"'The Morning! The Morning' I cried, 'I am caught by the morning and I am a ghost.' But it was too late." (p. 145)		- George MacDonald

 ©2010, 2017. Wheaton Press™ All Rights Reserved.

The Great Divorce

Some Facts to remember as you interact with the story

- This information is taken from the book Images of Salvation in the Fiction of C. S. Lewis by Clyde S. Kilby; Harold Shaw Publishers, Wheaton IL, 1978. (Pages 83-85)

1. In the eighteenth century William Blake had written a poem called "The Marriage of Heaven and Hell." Lewis' story, on the other hand, endeavors to represent heaven and hell as far removed from each other, with vast differences between them.

2. The main intent of the story is not to suggest a second chance of salvation nor to propound abstract doctrines about heaven and hell (the narrative is actually presented in the form of a dream) but simply to affirm that people go to hell because they choose not to give up themselves. It is best summarized in Macdonald's remark: "There are only two kinds of people in the end: those who say to God, 'Thy will be done.' And those to whom God says, in the end, 'Thy will be done.' All that are in Hell, choose it" (Chapter IX). Thus, it is a story about that constant called the Self, which is operative, moment by moment, in every person's life.

3. Interestingly, all but one of the bus-riders are guilty of "respectable" sins (Ones we may generally find at WA or Church) such as love of money, cynicism, gossip, overwrought ambition, misguided intellect, self-importance and the substitution of legalistic morality for Christianity. The only traveler who gives himself up to be changed is guilty of the "bad" sin of lust. In the next to the last chapter of Mere Christianity Lewis reiterates his warning against the "respectable" sins that may be the worst ones.

4. Going to hell is not represented as a cataclysmic event as it was for Faust when a man was suddenly tricked into helplessness. Nor is it seen as a deliberate and reasoned decision. Rather it is the culmination of a series of "insignificant" daily acts and choices which push one further and further from Reality, until the time comes when, one finds himself so far down the road to destruction that his choice must almost inevitably follow the course of the rut it has hollowed for itself.

5. One of the values of this story is the sharpening of our normally dull and hazy concepts of both hell and heaven. Hell here is seen as ghostly, quarrelsome and eternally drab, but heaven is made so real that in it men appear like ghosts. Even the furthest glimpse of heaven is one of ineluctable glory. Even the vegetation of heaven is too much for hell.

6. But heaven is by no means simply a place of beatitude and passivity. Rather it is where one actively grows up "into a Person." It is a place of diversity of gift, and its watchword is "farther in and higher up," always in the direction of "Deep Heaven." (Chapter IX).

7. As usual, Lewis suggests that negative experiences may open one's spiritual eyes as much as positive ones. Thus the murderer thinking of the horror and shame of his deed is brought to repentance. *[Christ will redeem our pain and shame if we let him! And we should; He is really good at redeeming things!]*

©2010, 2017. Wheaton Press™ All Rights Reserved.

The Great Divorce

Some facts to remember as you interact with the story:

- This information is taken from the book Images of Salvation in the Fiction of C. S. Lewis by Clyde S. Kilby; Harold Shaw Publishers, Wheaton IL, 1978. (Pages 83-85)

8. Charles William's concept of heavenly "co-inherence" is illustrated by its opposite in this story, for in hell the people are pictured as constantly moving farther and farther from each other until some are astronomical distances apart.

9. Lewis, as always, denigrates liberalism in religion. His image of the Episcopal Bishop is a personified summary of his many comments on this subject. On the other hand, he confirms his belief in Biblical realities such as the following:
- Christ is "the Bleeding Charity" (IV)
- Before God no man has any "rights" (V)
- The Resurrection (V)
- Heaven is not the place of questions but of answers of "Eternal Fact" (V)
- "Crude Salvationism," and repentance and becoming "white as snow" (V)
- Shame, one of the most difficult experiences of our lives to endure, is recommended as healthy. "Drink the cup of shame to its dregs, says he, and you will find it nourishing" (VIII).
- Each must submit to death to himself or herself (XI)

10. George Mac Donald, the nineteenth-century writer and theologian who, more than any other, influenced Lewis, is introduced into the story as one of heaven's glorified saints. He is a guide and teacher and instructs the onlooker (Lewis himself) on a broad range of topics. He reminds him, for instance, that even a spiritual man may become so interested in his dogmatics, such as the proof of God's existence, that he loses his real love for God Himself (IX); that beings in the natural universe are good as they look to God and bad as they turn away from him; and the higher and mightier a thing is in the natural order, "the more demonic it will be if it rebels."

11. Lewis always clearly shows the difference between sentimentalized affection and the strong, firm love which is of God. Indeed, he implies that love for God must precede any genuine love for a fellow creature (XII).

12. Of course this book consistently presents a strong case for man's free will. One must consciously make, not postpone, a choice to be Christ's. "This moment contains all moments" (XI).

13. Lewis never presents salvation as an easy or painless matter. In his autobiography he related his own dreadful experience of having to get down on his knees before God and confess his sins and give up himself. In this story the lustful man had first to come to the point of being willing to have "the old man" in him destroyed and then accept suffering prior to the great joy which was given him (XI).

14. As usual, Lewis ends his story on a note of great joy. We see Sarah Smith as a nobody on earth but now celebrated as a queen in heaven, and we learn that she is now in Love (XIII). She has attained the quiet and permanent ecstasy which also surrounds the Green Lady in Perelandra.

The Great Divorce: A song to ponder and discuss:

"Shadowfeet" By Brooke Frasier
Be sure to check out the the lyrics and the YouTube video
https://www.youtube.com/watch?v=Y4KiGN1j1No

 ©2010, 2017. Wheaton Press™ All Rights Reserved.

Notes 13/13

Quiz on *The Great Divorce*: Preface and Chapters 1-3

Please answer true or false for the statements below.

1) **F** When the book opens it is sunny and the middle of the day.

2) **F** "Queue" means road or pathway; journey.

3) **F** The narrator said that the Bookshops in the grey town had the book The Republic by Plato.

4) **T** The Driver was full of Light and confident.

5) **T** The Bus can fly.

6) **F** The majority of the people the narrator meets in the Grey Town are generous and kind.

7) **F** When neighbors quarrel in the "grey town" they work hard at resolving their disagreements.

8) **F** The "Intelligent man" feels secure and safe in the "grey town".

9) **T** The "Tousle-Headed Poet" had killed himself for several reasons, but particularly lack of recognition, and he was hoping to find recognition and appreciation at this place where the Driver was taking him.

10) **T** The people in the "grey town" can have whatever they want by simply thinking it. In essence it seems as though they have no real Needs.

11) **T** Lewis believes that "If we insist on keeping Hell (or even Earth) we shall not see Heaven…"

12) **F** In this book Lewis specifically wants to give us what he believes to be the Theologically True picture of Heaven.

13) In the space below, clearly explain a parallel between the opening chapters of The Great Divorce and Plato's allegory of the cave.

In the opening chapter, all characters are all live in the shadow and they do not know they are not live in the real world

©2010, 2017. Wheaton Press™ All Rights Reserved. 127

Philosophy & Theology

NOTES on "HOW TO READ" *The Great Divorce*, Preface and Chapters 1-3

Please answer <u>True</u> or <u>False</u> for the statements below. (Is the statement correct?)
- *Please correct the questions as we go through them; take notes on how to read the book. The teacher will use each of these questions as "Tips" on how to make some sense of these crazy unique and profound opening chapters…*
- *Generally, people put this book down before they really get to the meat in chapters 4 and following because they get lost in how to read it. Unfortunately, people miss out on this book because they miss the allegory of the cave allusion, and the concept of false self and true self, the battle between the kingdom of darkness and light, and the tension between the invitation to joy and the false security in fear and shadows… Like Screwtape Letters, if you do not know how to read the book you will quickly become unsettled and confused. Like Screwtape Letters, if you can figure out what is going on it is immensely profound.*

1) ___F___ When the book opens it is sunny and the middle of the day.
TIP: SETTING MATTERS – *keep an eye on time and setting it is twilight in the opening chapters, and just before dawn in the later chapters. It is not fully dark in the grey town; it is not fully light in the solid country: the setting lends itself to be like earth – we are somewhere in the middle between heaven and hell.*

2) ___F___ "Queue" means road or pathway; journey.
TIP: LOOK UP WORDS YOU DO NOT KNOW! *First, he is British ☺; second, he is a literary genius and an Oxford scholar; third, he does not waste words… This is a piece of literature; most of the words are loaded with multiple meanings and highly intentional. Finally, it takes about 30 seconds to look up a word you do not know (thanks Siri). Please do not read an entire chapter about the "Apostate Ghost" and never look up the word apostasy…*

3) ___F___ The narrator said that the Bookshops in the grey town had the book The Republic by Plato.
TIP: This is a book about philosophy and the nature of reality (a topic near and dear to Lewis' heart), and Lewis will make many philosophical references. *This detail keys the reader into the fact that he is talking about the contrast between Plato and Aristotle on the nature of reality and the interaction between the material and spiritual realms. Furthermore, this is literature – DETAILS MATTER and more often then not the details have layers of meaning.*

4) ___T___ The Driver was full of Light and confident. *Jesus as the driver of the bus is the light and way*
TIP: CHARACTER DEVELOPMENT IS CRITICAL; & THE CAPITALIZATION IS INTENTIONAL. *Keep in mind that these characters are on a journey and Lewis spends the opening chapters developing their character. Note that he is also using the literary/poetic technique of capitalization for meaning. When a word is capitalized like Driver, this is not just any driver, he is THE Driver (of the universe…) and it is not just any light, it is THE Light (of the World). Have fun with this throughout the book. Your tip is that this is to be particularly noticed when it is not at the beginning of a sentence. (Extend your learning and look up Sign Semiotics: Signified and Signifiers with Ferdinand De Saussure on the web!)*

5) ___T___ The Bus can fly. *Lewis & details matter a lot*
TIP: USE YOUR IMAGINATION! *This is what Lewis himself called an "imaginative supposal" – What if Jesus drove a flying bus Down to hell? What if He took a bunch of souls up to Heaven and offered them a chance to stay? What if they had that choice to leave Hell and Choose Heaven? What would they choose to do? WHAT IF? – Use your imagination – or this book will not work. Samuel Taylor Coleridge called this a "willing suspension of disbelief." It allows us to enter into a creative story and the creative process without getting hung up on the particulars… "Suspension of disbelief or willing suspension of disbelief is a term coined in 1817 by the poet and aesthetic philosopher Samuel Taylor Coleridge, who suggested that if a writer could infuse "human interest and a semblance of truth" into a fantastic tale, the reader would suspend judgment concerning the implausibility of the narrative.*

128   ©2010, 2017. Wheaton Press™ All Rights Reserved.

NOTES on "HOW TO READ" *The Great Divorce*, Preface and Chapters 1-3

NOTE: Questions 6-10 are specifically designed to discuss the fact that this book can be read as though these "conversations and invitations" between the shadows and the solid people are all taking place here on earth. These questions when looked at in a certain light paint a picture of our churches and neighborhoods…

These are conversations that if we are solid in our faith and identity we can be having with people that Jesus drops off in front of us each day. Or if we are a bit shadowy, they are conversations that we get to have with the solid people that the driver of our destinies steers us towards. It is about the invitation out of the shadows into the Kingdom of God here and now. This is "door" #2. ("Thy Kingdom come here on Earth as it is in Heaven…")

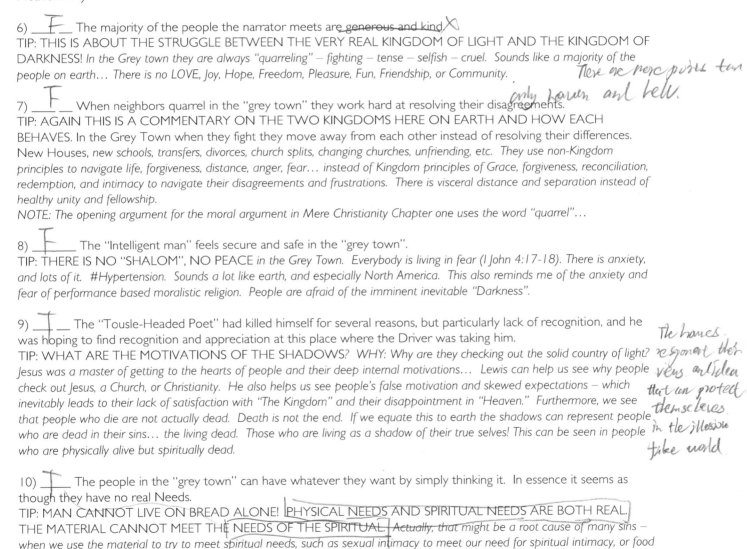

6) __F__ The majority of the people the narrator meets are ~~generous and kind~~ X
TIP: THIS IS ABOUT THE STRUGGLE BETWEEN THE VERY REAL KINGDOM OF LIGHT AND THE KINGDOM OF DARKNESS! *In the Grey town they are always "quarreling" – fighting – tense – selfish – cruel. Sounds like a majority of the people on earth… There is no LOVE, Joy, Hope, Freedom, Pleasure, Fun, Friendship, or Community.*

There are more places than only heaven and hell.

7) __F__ When neighbors quarrel in the "grey town" they work hard at resolving their disagreements.
TIP: AGAIN THIS IS A COMMENTARY ON THE TWO KINGDOMS HERE ON EARTH AND HOW EACH BEHAVES. In the Grey Town when they fight they move away from each other instead of resolving their differences. New Houses, *new schools, transfers, divorces, church splits, changing churches, unfriending, etc. They use non-Kingdom principles to navigate life, forgiveness, distance, anger, fear… instead of Kingdom principles of Grace, forgiveness, reconciliation, redemption, and intimacy to navigate their disagreements and frustrations. There is visceral distance and separation instead of healthy unity and fellowship.*
NOTE: *The opening argument for the moral argument in Mere Christianity Chapter one uses the word "quarrel"…*

8) __F__ The "Intelligent man" feels secure and safe in the "grey town".
TIP: THERE IS NO "SHALOM", NO PEACE *in the Grey Town. Everybody is living in fear (I John 4:17-18). There is anxiety, and lots of it. #Hypertension. Sounds a lot like earth, and especially North America. This also reminds me of the anxiety and fear of performance based moralistic religion. People are afraid of the imminent inevitable "Darkness".*

9) __T__ The "Tousle-Headed Poet" had killed himself for several reasons, but particularly lack of recognition, and he was hoping to find recognition and appreciation at this place where the Driver was taking him.
TIP: WHAT ARE THE MOTIVATIONS OF THE SHADOWS? WHY: *Why are they checking out the solid country of light?* *The homes resonant their views and idea that can protect themselves in the illusion like world* *Jesus was a master of getting to the hearts of people and their deep internal motivations… Lewis can help us see why people check out Jesus, a Church, or Christianity. He also helps us see people's false motivation and skewed expectations – which inevitably leads to their lack of satisfaction with "The Kingdom" and their disappointment in "Heaven." Furthermore, we see that people who die are not actually dead. Death is not the end. If we equate this to earth the shadows can represent people who are dead in their sins… the living dead. Those who are living as a shadow of their true selves! This can be seen in people who are physically alive but spiritually dead.*

10) __T__ The people in the "grey town" can have whatever they want by simply thinking it. In essence it seems as though they have no real Needs.
TIP: MAN CANNOT LIVE ON BREAD ALONE! PHYSICAL NEEDS AND SPIRITUAL NEEDS ARE BOTH REAL. THE MATERIAL CANNOT MEET THE NEEDS OF THE SPIRITUAL. *Actually, that might be a root cause of many sins – when we use the material to try to meet spiritual needs, such as sexual intimacy to meet our need for spiritual intimacy, or food for our need for our spiritual daily "bread", or physical pleasure trying to meet the need for spiritual joy… The material realm can only meet our material needs, and the material realm is transient and passing: matter and electricity, dust. Ironically, many students think that this is the point that is least like earth; however I remind them that many of them thought about the next upgrade a month before it "shows up" for their phone. Or the truth that I used to type my papers on a typewriter… and now look at laptops. But it all does not last and it cannot meet our spiritual needs.*

©2010, 2017. Wheaton Press™ All Rights Reserved.

NOTES on "HOW TO READ" *The Great Divorce*, Preface and Chapters 1-3

11) __ L __ Lewis believes that "If we insist on keeping Hell (or even Earth) we shall not see Heaven…"

TIP: A MAIN THEME OF THIS BOOK IS FREE WILL and FREEDOM! *Lewis is inviting us into a greater understanding of the richness of the freedom offered to us in Christ. We are free from our sin and we are free not to sin. On this topic the scenes in this book paint a vivid picture of the opportunity we have to experience the Lord's Prayer. "Thy Kingdom Come" is not simply words to recite – it is a request for The King's Dominion to start here and now on our journey, not just when we go further up and further in through the door of death. We get to play a hand in that if we are willing to surrender our will to His when we submit and say "Thy will be done on earth as it is in Heaven." I anecdotally share this by walking across the front of my classroom towards Heaven… I tell my students that "I am Sealed for the Day of Redemption" and that "nothing can separate me from God's Love" and I mention that I could continue in sin such as lying or pride or a religious spirit as I walk towards the door of death. Then I bump into the door and realize that none of that is allowed in The King's Domain – The KINGDOM of Heaven. So I will need to leave it behind at the door; death and some Holy Spirit Fire cleanse me of these death giving, life destroying vices and I enter Eternal Fellowship with my Heavenly Father. I then pause and point out that if we read this book with a careful eye and creative imagination, Lewis, when writing about our Journey on Earth, is actually imploring us not just wait till death to let go of our sinful, shadowy, destructive behaviors and lifestyles, do it NOW. Choose this day whom you will serve, embrace your freedom here and now. I phrase it like this: since you have to let them go eventually, you might as well let go of it now; that might be one of the multitudinous meanings of Thy Kingdom Come. "If the Son has Set you Free, you are Free indeed!" We need to believe it and live it here and now.*

12) ___ F ___ In this book Lewis specifically wants to give us what he believes to be the Theologically True picture of Heaven.

TIP: NO! NO! NO! NO! HE SAYS SO HIMSELF AT THE END OF HIS OWN INTRODUCTION TO THE TEXT. *"The second thing is this. I beg readers to remember that this is a fantasy. It has of course—or I intended it to have—a moral. But the trans-mortal conditions are solely an imaginative supposal: they are not even a guess or a speculation at what may actually await us. The last thing I wish is to arouse factual curiosity about the details of the after-world.*

C. S. LEWIS April, 1945" This is a piece of literature, and must be handled as such. It is littered with scriptural references and imagery on every page, however it is not a Biblical or doctrinal commentary in the traditional sense. He calls this literary structure an "imaginative supposal" – something he is famous for. It goes something like this: Imagine if Jesus were to graciously take a big gold bus to hell and pick up people who might be interested in Heaven. Imagine if He drove them to the porch of heaven and said they could freely stay as long as they wanted to (ch. 3). Imagine if these shadowy unbelieving characters were to be invited to stay and be transformed into new creatures. The invitation comes in the form of authentic dialogue between the curious shadows and loving believers who were solid in their faith, identity, and character. What would these visitors from hell choose? Would they stay and be transformed or go back to the shadows? What would motivate someone to stay? When leaving, what is motivating a shadowy character to reject a loving, open, gracious, compelling invitation to stay in Heaven? Lewis powerfully offers us a picture of a Gracious, open-armed God who freely invites all to be transformed and enter heaven; the ones in this story who are in hell are there by his or her own choice… (This imaginative supposal is also seen in the Screwtape Letters. Imagine if a young tempter demon were to get mentoring letters from an experienced diabolical tempter on how to best tempt and destroy a human. The Chronicles of Narnia are built off of this concept, particularly the Lion the Witch and the Wardrobe. Imagine if a world of talking animals need to be saved from an evil sorceress. Imagine that God chose to save them himself and he appeared in the world of Narnia in the form of a Lion…)

13) On this page: Clearly explain a parallel between the opening chapters of The Great Divorce and Plato's "Allegory of the Cave".

TIP: THIS MISUNDERSTOOD CONCEPT IS OFTEN WHY MANY PEOPLE DO NOT MAKE IT PAST THE FIRST FEW CHAPTERS BEFORE CONFUSEDLY GIVING UP ON THE BOOK. UNFORTUNATELY THEY MISS OUT ON THE TREASURES THAT ARE FOUND IN CHAPTER 3 AND BEYOND. *This is ripe for open discussion. Flip back to the beginning of this "Thinkbook" and look at your notes on the Allegory of the cave. The land of shadow, the painful conversion, being "disabused of their errors", the REAL world is solid and beautiful, the world of Light is compelling and filled with truth, goodness, and beauty… the list goes on.*

Learning Assessment
Character Profile from *The Great Divorce*: A Shadow

Name: _____   Class: _____

Choose a shadowy character from the text and fill out the following profile for him or her. Use complete sentences. Be clear and concise.

Chapter(s) used in profile: 4   5   6   7   8   9   10   11   12   13

Shadowy Character: _____

1) Please describe your shadowy character in detail: personality, clothing, size, language, occupation, emotional attributes, spirituality, actions, behavior, etc.

2) Describe the solid person (solid spirit), if there is one, who comes to visit this shadowy character.

3) What is the main issue (sin) that your shadowy character is struggling with? Explain how this sin affects the character, what he or she believes, how he or she views the world, and how he or she is behaving.

Learning Assessment
Character Profile from *The Great Divorce*: A Shadow

4) Why did your shadowy character come to the Solid Country? What is motivating him or her to check things out?

5) What is your shadowy character's final choice (to stay or leave)? Why does he or she make this choice?

4) If your character leaves, or would leave, what does he or she specifically need to do in order to be able to stay? If he or she stayed, what did he or she specifically do in order to stay?

5) Select and write out at least two quotes from *The Great Divorce* that directly apply to your shadowy character's profile.

6) Write out or describe two Bible verses/passages that directly relate to what you have developed in this character profile.

 ©2010, 2017. Wheaton Press™ All Rights Reserved.

Learning Assessment
Character Profile from *The Great Divorce*: A Solid Person

Name: _____   Class: _____

Choose a solid character from the text and fill out the following profile for him or her. Use complete sentences. Be clear and concise.

Chapter(s) used in profile: 4   5   6   7   8   9   10   11   12   13

Solid Character: _____

1) Please describe your solid character in detail: personality, clothing, size, language, occupation, emotional attributes, spirituality, actions, behavior, etc.

2) What are some key aspects of love as seen in 1 Corinthians 13 and some fruits of the spirit that are overtly evident in this solid person's behavior and character?

3) Briefly describe the shadowy character that this solid person is inviting into the kingdom.

©2010, 2017. Wheaton Press™ All Rights Reserved.   133

Learning Assessment
Character Profile from *The Great Divorce*: A Solid Person

4) How is the solid character specifically treating the shadowy character? What questions are asked? What is the tone and language used? What is his or her main method for inviting the shadow to stay in the kingdom?

5) If your shadowy character leaves, or would leave, how does the solid person respond in the moment of departure?

6) Select and write out at least two quotes from *The Great Divorce* that directly apply to your solid character's profile.

7) Write out or describe two Bible verses/passages that directly relate to what you have developed in this solid character's profile.

 ©2010, 2017. Wheaton Press™ All Rights Reserved.

All Sin is Warped Good
The man with the lizard

"Every good and perfect gift is from above, coming down from the Father of the heavenly lights, who does not change like shifting shadows." (James 1:17)

"The thief comes only to steal and kill and destroy; I have come that they may have life, and have it to the full." (John 10:10)

"In order that in the coming ages he might show the incomparable riches of his grace, expressed in his kindness to us in Christ Jesus. For it is by grace you have been saved, through faith—and this is not from yourselves, it is the gift of God—not by works, so that no one can boast." (Ephesians 2:7-9)

The warped good (sin) **Broken, twisted, perverted**		**The good and perfect gift** **The full life (virtue)**
1) Gossip *(is a warped use of…)*	1)	
2) Teasing / Bullying / Put-Downs *(is warped…)*	2)	
3) Being Judgmental *(is a warped version of…)*	3)	
4) Mocking others *(is warped…)*	4)	
5) The Religious Spirit *(is a warped version of…)*	5)	
6)	6)	
7)	7)	
8)	8)	

Further analysis and application:

- Idealism: How can this all fit (especially the verses) into the practical life of an Idealist—a person who is trying to achieve perfection and escape this world of warped good?

- Theism: We often suffer from the lack of a model for good in our teenage culture. What is one area where this is true? Come up with a strategy to be a culture-maker for this issue. In light of this concept, what are some specific ways we can offer hope to people drowning in sin?

- Materialism and monism: What specific problems do these philosophies face if this concept of evil and sin is actually a true picture of reality?

©2010, 2017. Wheaton Press™ All Rights Reserved.

All Sin is Warped Good
Lessons on Killing the Lizard

"Put to death, therefore, whatever belongs to your earthly nature."
(Colossians 3:5)

An Non-Exhaustive List of Lessons on Killing the Lizard
(not a system and not a progression)

1) Identity — get to the core sin; go to the source, not just the symptoms. You need to get the roots of the sin like pulling weeds out of the ground.
2) Understand—the nature and fruit of sin. Sin is evil, and sin bears evil fruit. Sin brings death; it is not just bad or a perspective. Stop rationalizing. Sin grows out of our desires.
3) Desire—freedom from your sin. Really want the sin dead!
4) Be Honest—with yourself and others. Admit that you need help—especially God's help. Receive help from God and His body of truly grace-filled believers.
5) Confess—your sin to God and trusted loved ones. Repent.
6) Forgiveness—ask for it when needed and seek reconciliation and restoration.
7) Ask —God and people you trust for help. Sin will not die unless Christ kills it. Know that He already has killed your sin, and get help from His body (the church) to move past it.
8) Receive—help and be willing to let the sin go and seek accountability, therapy, or mentoring. Let the Holy Spirit change who you are. Put on your new self.
9) Remove—yourself from the temptation and remove the temptation from yourself. Read the book of Proverbs.
10) Remember—in Christ you are a new creation. When Christ kills sin it is dead. There is victory. However, you do need to block the sin from growing new roots. Your identity is massively important (Romans 5-8).
11) Close—any doors or windows that might be open to the enemy. Take away the footholds. Consider the spiritual components of the battles with sin.
12) Understand—that all sin is warped good. Sin is a parasite. Sin is a shadow. Your attraction to sin will not die if you do not believe it is a lesser option. You need to truly and wholeheartedly believe sin is a secondary and destructive lifestyle or you will keep going back to it.
13) Acknowledge and identify—the valid physical, emotional, and spiritual needs you are trying to satisfy through your sin. What is motivating you both consciously and subconsciously? What is the purpose of/behind your behavior? What are the legitimate reasons you are drawn to your sin?
14) Find—the good that your sin gets its life from.
15) Create—your own model/understanding of the good based on God's truth if you need to. Renew your mind and heart. Truth kills lies.
16) Believe—that God's way to live (the real good) is the best way to live. Trust that it is better than the sin. Change your focus.
17) Completely—destroy the sin. It needs to be all or nothing. Know that is has been destroyed and is destroyed
18) Replace—the warped good with the real good. Fill your desires to satisfy your needs with the real good.
19) Live—richly, freely, and wisely. Live the full life.
20) Live—joyful and graceful lives.

 ©2010, 2017. Wheaton Press™ All Rights Reserved.

Scripture Reading Integrity Assignments
James and *The Great Divorce*

Read and annotate the letter of James written by James, the brother of Jesus, as an essay in one sitting. Pretend you are a member of the church. Where do you see connections to our discussion on *The Great Divorce*, particularly on killing sin? The connections you make can be subtle, overt, literary, historical, artistic, personal, or metaphoric.

In the space below, write down at least three verses that you find engaging, and briefly explain why you picked these verses. Cut and paste or write out the entire verse, but do not simply put the reference. Do not summarize the verse as a response.

Artwork courtesy of JSD

©2010, 2017. Wheaton Press™ All Rights Reserved.

Philosophy & Theology

"Further Up and Further In!" - The Last Battle

Seeds for discussion and journal responses:

1. Puzzle: Why is all of this deception and manipulation regarding the lion skin happening to Puzzle? What could he do to prevent this? What is missing in his life to help him in this situation? How Does Puzzle Feel?

The Last Battle From the end of Chapter 1:
"Well, stand still then," said the Ape. The skin was very heavy for him to lift, but in the end, with a lot of pulling and pushing and puffing and blowing, he got it onto the donkey. He tied it underneath Puzzle's body and he tied the legs to Puzzle's legs and the tail to Puzzle's tail. A good deal of Puzzle's gray nose and face could be seen through the open mouth of the lion's head. No one who had ever seen a real lion would have been taken in for a moment. But if someone who had never seen a lion looked at Puzzle in his lion-skin he just might mistake him for a lion, if he didn't come too close, and if the light was not too good, and if Puzzle didn't let out a bray and didn't make any noise with his hoofs."
"You look wonderful, wonderful," said the Ape. "If anyone saw you now, they'd think you were Aslan, the Great Lion, himself."
"That would be dreadful," said Puzzle.
"No it wouldn't," said Shift. "Everyone would do whatever you told them."
"But I don't want to tell them anything."
"But you think of the good we could do!" said Shift. "You'd have me to advise you, you know. I'd think of sensible orders for you to give. And everyone would have to obey us, even the King himself. We would set everything right in Narnia."
"But isn't everything right already?" said Puzzle.
"What!" cried Shift. "Everything right—when there are no oranges or bananas?"
"Well, you know," said Puzzle, "there aren't many people—in fact, I don't think there's anyone but yourself—who wants those sort of things."
"There's sugar too," said Shift.
"H'm, yes," said the Ass. "It would be nice if there was more sugar."
"Well then, that's settled," said the Ape. You will pretend to be Aslan, and I'll tell you what to say."
"No, no, no," said Puzzle. "Don't say such dreadful things. It would be wrong, Shift. I may be not very clever but I know that much. What would become of us if the real Aslan turned up?"
"I expect he'd be very pleased," said Shift. "Probably he sent us the lion-skin on purpose, so that we could set things to right. Anyway, he never does turn up, you know. Not nowadays."
At that moment there came a great thunderclap right overhead and the ground trembled with a small earthquake. Both the animals lost their balance and were flung on their faces.
"There!" gasped Puzzle, as soon as he "
"had breath to speak. "It's a sign, a warning. I knew we were doing something dreadfully wicked. Take this wretched skin off me at once."
"No, no," said the Ape (whose mind worked very quickly). "It's a sign the other way. I was just going to say that if the real Aslan, as you call him, meant us to go on with this, he would send us a thunderclap and an earth-tremor. It was just on the tip of my tongue, only the sign itself came before I could get the words out. You've got to do it now, Puzzle. And please don't let us have any more arguing. You know you don't understand these things. What could a donkey know about signs?"

2. All great stories point to the true great story: Where is this happening in our story or in our history? At school? At your church? What is the difference between Tash and Aslan?

 ©2010, 2017. Wheaton Press™ All Rights Reserved.

"Further Up and Further In!" - The Last Battle

Seeds for discussion and journal responses:

3. How would you respond? How do different characters respond? What does this reveal about their character?

4. The centaur dies! People are dying: What would you die for? What is worth dying for? List three things and explain why they are worth dying for.

5. How does who we trust affect our interpretation of reality and our surroundings? King Tirian is trusting specific individuals to interpret what is going on, and that affects how he responds. Trust list!

Notes and additional thoughts:

- Ch. 1 Puzzle to the Ape: "I don't think it would honor Aslan."
- Ch. 1 Ape: Prophecy after the fact = red flag.
- Ch. 2 Desecration of your history… the trees. The foundation! Aslan would not do this!
- Ch. 2 The stars… hold on for sure. Bible and General Revelation etc.
- Ch. 3 The false mouth piece for Aslan…
- Ch. 3 The Ape to the Bear: "True freedom is doing what I tell you."
- Consider Intimacy with Aslan (talk with Aslan), encounter, try to convince Lucy it would not happen.

"Further Up and Further In!" - The Last Battle

Seeds for discussion and journal responses:

6.   Emeth: "Encounter!" Aslan moment. What service did unto Tash I receive unto me.... Puzzle's encounter - his Aslan moment. No shame. #encounter

"Then I fell at his feet and thought, Surely this is the hour of death, for the Lion (who is worthy of all honor) will know that I have served Tash all my days and not him. Nevertheless, it is better to see the Lion and die then to be Tisroc of the world and live and not to have seen him. But the Glorious One bent down his golden head and touched my forehead with his tongue and said, Son, thou art welcome. But I said, Alas, Lord, I am no son of thine but the servant of Tash. He answered Child, all the service thou has done to Tash, I account as service done to me. Then by reasons of my great desire for wisdom and understanding, I overcame my fear and questioned the Glorious One and said, Lord, is it true, as the Ape said, that thou and Tash are one? The Lion growled so that the earth shook (but his wrath was not against me) and said, It is false. Not because he and I are one, but because we are opposites, I take to me the services which thou hast done to him. For I and he are of such different kinds that no service which is vile can be done to me, and none which is not vile can be done to him. Therefore if any man swear by Tash and keep his oath for the oath's sake, it is by me that he has truly sworn, though he know it not, and it is I who reward him. And if any man do cruelty in my name, then, though he says the name Aslan, it is Tash whom he serves and by Tash his deed accepted. Dost though understand, Child? I said Lord, thou knows how much I understand. But I said also (for the truth constrained me), Yet I have been seeking Tash all my days. Beloved, said the Glorious One, unless thy desire had been for me thou would not have sought so long and so truly. For all find what they truly seek. Then he breathed upon me and took away the trembling of my limbs and caused me to stand on my feet. And after that, he said not much but that we should meet again, and I must go further up and further in. Then he turned him about and in a storm and flurry of gold and was gone suddenly. And since then, O Kings and Ladies, I have been wandering to find him and my happiness is so great that it even weakens me like a wound. And this is the marvel of marvels, that he called me Beloved, me who am but as a dog..."

#HecalledmeBeloved
From Emeth in The Last Battle by C. S. Lewis. (pg. 188-189)

     ©2010, 2017. Wheaton Press™ All Rights Reserved.

"Further Up and Further In!" - The Last Battle Ch. 12-16:

Seeds for discussion and journal responses:

7.   Ironically and painfully much of this reminds me of the unique situation that the Dwarves are in at the ending of The Last Battle in the Narnia series by Lewis. These dwarves are sitting in a beautiful green field next to the kings and queens of Narnia end even Aslan himself, yet they see it as dark, the food is rank, and the ground is uncomfortable. Here is a taste of that passage.

"The sweet air grew suddenly sweeter. A brightness flashed behind them. All turned. Tirian turned last because he was afraid. There stood his heart's desire, huge and real, the golden Lion, Aslan himself, and already the others were kneeling in a circle round his forepaws and burying their hands and faces in his mane as he stooped his great head to touch them with his tongue. Then he fixed his eyes upon Tirian, and Tirian came near, trembling, and flung himself at the Lion's feet, and the Lion kissed him and said, "Well done, last of the Kings of Narnia who stood firm at the darkest hour."

"Aslan," said Lucy through her tears, "could you—will you—do something for these poor Dwarfs?"

"Dearest," said Aslan, "I will show you both what I can, and what I cannot, do." He came close to the Dwarfs and gave a low growl: low, but it set all the air shaking. But the Dwarfs said to one another, "Hear that? That's the gang at the other end of the stable. Trying to frighten us. They do it with a machine of some kind. Don't take any notice. They won't take us in again!"

Aslan raised his head and shook his mane. Instantly a glorious feast appeared on the Dwarfs' knees: pies and tongues and pigeons and trifles and ices, and each Dwarf had a goblet of good wine in his right hand. But it wasn't much use. They began eating and drinking greedily enough, but it was clear that they couldn't taste it properly. They thought they were eating and drinking only the sort of things you might find in a stable. One said he was trying to eat hay and another said he had got a bit of an old turnip and a third said he'd found a raw cabbage leaf. And they raised golden goblets of rich red wine to their lips and said "Ugh! Fancy drinking dirty water out of a trough that a donkey's been at! Never thought we'd come to this.' But very soon every Dwarf began suspecting that every other Dwarf had found something nicer than he had, and they started grabbing and snatching, and went on to quarreling, till in a few minutes there was a free fight and all the good food was smeared on their faces and clothes or trodden under foot. But when at last they sat down to nurse their black eyes and their bleeding noses, they all said:

"Well, at any rate there's no Humbug here. We haven't let anyone take us in. The Dwarfs are for the Dwarfs."

"You see," said Aslan. "They will not let us help them. They have chosen cunning instead of belief. Their prison is only in their own minds, yet they are in that prison; and so afraid of being taken in that they cannot be taken out. But come, children. I have other work to do." (184-186).

8.   Further up and further in - to what? What do you need to leave behind in order to move forward.
      Intimacy. Love.

9.   What is our true identity? Kings and queens in Narnia! (Shadowlands)

10. Narnia fades, all things fade, it all should point us to the truth: all are pictures and all are on a journey...
     Do not substitute the means for the end. It is all a journey to love, into love, for love, with love: it is all
     about Love!

©2010, 2017. Wheaton Press™ All Rights Reserved. 141

Discerning the Spirits (I John Chapter 4)
"Harmony, Unity, Family, and Spiritual Gifts!" The Body of Christ.
Quotes, notes, doodles, and discussion

A tool for the living the "Most Excellent Way"

Artwork public domain

    ©2010, 2017. Wheaton Press™ All Rights Reserved.

Extra Pages for Quotes, Notes, Doodles, and Discussions

"Testing the Spirits"

Some Essential Scriptures:
The Gospels, I John 4 (verse 4*) "the anchor!", I Corinthians 12 & 13, Galatians 5, Ephesians 6, The Book of Acts, Romans 5, 6, 7, 8! 2 Timothy 3:16 & 17, Hebrews 4:12, Isaiah 61/Matthew 4:18&19, Matthew 28:18-20, Luke 7:22&23/Matthew 11:5&6, James 3:13-18!

+ Biblical Truth.
+ Extra Biblical Truth. (General Revelation)
+ New Testament Prophecy = God's Word = "My Sheep hear my Voice!"
- Warped use of scripture = lies and misused truth; toxic theology, toxic doctrine
(Satan used scripture to tempt Jesus)
- Extra Biblical Lies.
- Anti Biblical = Not Truth.
- Anti Christ = Against Jesus and Against the Power of the Holy Spirit

SPIRITS TO TEST (This is not Monism!)
- Holy Spirit
- Angels
- Demons (corrupted angels)
- New Human Spirit
- Dead Human Spirit
- "Other Spirits" #Mystery

4 Scenarios for Discussion and to practice using the tool:
- "Demon next door…"
- Resurrection from the dead: "There will be NO funeral today"
- Spontaneous Supernatural Healing
- Signs and wonders: "Glory Cloud, Gold Dust, Food Multiplying, Changing the Weather, Provision of Money"

"My Sheep know My Voice!"
God still communicates with humans especially Spirit to spirit, but He will not be antithetical to the voice of His word as recorded in Scripture. The Comforter/Helper will shepherd you, lead you, guide you, encourage you, and empower you. It is essential that you get to know and trust His voice! Remember: The Voices you give permission and power to influence you will shape you and your perspectives of God, God's followers, yourself, the people around you, and your world view.

Voices you can give authority to:
God's Voice! This voice will NEVER be antithetical to his Character and his Word as recorded in Scripture and seen in Jesus.
Your New Self – with The Mind of Christ!
Kingdom Voices in your life (Encouragement, rebukes, prophecy, love, life…)
Angels – God's Messengers
Your Dead Self's Voice
Voices of Darkness in your life
The Religious Spirit (Pharisees & Sadducees & "The Teachers of the Law" – not Grace!)
Demonic voices (Lies about you and God, fear, shame, guilt, condemnation)
"The System of this world"

©2010, 2017. Wheaton Press™ All Rights Reserved.

Philosophy & Theology

The "Aslan Moment": Quotes & Notes; Doodles & Discussions

List and describe as many "Aslan Moments" in the Chronicles of Narnia:
- Note the transformative power of each encounter...
- How is one moment different from another?
- What does each moment say about the concept of each of the characters in those stories being on an INDIVIDUAL Journey? And what does is say about Aslan's Timing for each Individual Character?
- How does Aslan's Quote to Shasta "Child,' said the Lion, 'I am telling you your story, not hers. No one is told any story but their own.'" in the Horse and His Boy reflect our need for a grace-filled and trusting understanding of God and His timing for individual encounters on each of our Journeys?

- EXAMPLES: Eustace and Aslan when Eustace is a Dragon; Edmund and Aslan after Edmund's Time with the White Witch; Lucy's ability to see Aslan when the others cannot see him...

 ©2010, 2017. Wheaton Press™ All Rights Reserved.

Scripture Reading Integrity Assignments
Galatians and *The Last Battle*

Read and annotate the letter to the church in Galatia written by Paul, as an essay in one sitting. Pretend you are a member of the church. Where do you see connections to our discussion on *The Last Battle*, particularly on the concept of "encounter"? The connections you make can be subtle, overt, literary, historical, artistic, personal, metaphoric, etc.

In the space below, write down at least three verses that you find engaging and briefly explain why you picked these verses. Cut and paste or write out the entire verse, do not simply put the reference. Do not summarize the verse as a response.

©2010, 2017. Wheaton Press™ All Rights Reserved.

©2010, 2017. Wheaton Press™ All Rights Reserved.

Unit 5
(ACT 5)

The Unfinished Story :
Life as Epic Mythic Adventure as
an Authentic Disciple of Christ.
The True Myth!

Philosophy & Theology

INVITED TO TRUST

UNIT 5 (Act 5) ESSENTIAL QUESTIONS:

1. What does it mean to see Life as a Journey?
2. What does it mean to see live as an epic adventure Journey
3. What is myth?
4. What is mythic literature (stories)?
5. How do all great stories point to the great True Story, What C.S. Lewis and J.J.R. Tolkien would call "the true myth"?
6. Why is it essential to see the Bible and particularly the book of Acts a the True Epic Adventure Story?
7. Why is it helpful (even essential) for me to see my life as an epic adventure journey?
8. What does it mean to live as an Authentic Disciple of Christ?

UNIT 5 (Act 5) READINGS:

1. Tolkien, J.R.R. *The Silmarillion* ("Ainundale" and "Valequenta")
2. *I Corinthians*
3. Tolkien, J.R.R. *The Hobbit* (Chapter 5, "Riddles in the Dark")
4. *Colossians*
5. Tolkien, J.R.R. *The Fellowship of the Ring*
6. *The Book of Acts*

UNIT 5 (Act 5) THINKBOOK LEARNING OPPORTUNITIES:

Formative:

- ❏ Annotations and Worksheet: *The Silmarillion* ("Ainundale" and "Valequenta")
- ❏ Scripture Reading "Truth Revealed": I Corinthians and *The Silmarillion*
- ❏ Annotations: "Riddles in the Dark"
- ❏ Scripture Reading "Truth Revealed": Colossians and *The Hobbit*
- ❏ *Objective Information and Reading Comprehension "quiz" on the book of ACTS*
- ❏ Scripture Reading "Truth Revealed": Acts and *The Fellowship of the Ring*

Summative:
- ❏ A Final Project: A Character Connection, A Quest, and My Quest
- ❏ A Post Assessment: The Philosophy Trust Lists Post-Assessment

UNIT 5 (Act 5) LEARNING PLAN:

1. Notes and discussion on Story, Myth, and The "True Myth"
2. *The Silmarillian* ("Ainundale" and "Valequenta")
2. *I Corinthians*
3. The Hobbit "Riddles in the Dark"
4. Colossians
5. Journey and Epic Adventure
6. *The Book of Acts Continues… "The True Epic Adventure Story"*
7. *My Life as Participating in the True Epic Adventure Journey!*

The True Myth: "All Great Stories Point to the True Great Story"

The "Unfinished Story":
The Lord's Prayer - thy kingdom come thy will be done on earth as it is in heaven.

Tolkien, Dyson, and C.S. Lewis on the famous Addison's Walk October 1931

"For Lewis some members of the Inklings, [their literary discussion group,] were also important for his transformation form an atheist to a theist to a Christian. From about the age of ten to about the age of thirty three he, [C.S. Lewis], had been assuming that Christianity was just another myth, a beautiful lie. He was the most reluctant convert in the United Kingdom, he didn't really want to be a believer. But he couldn't help himself; he was drawn to God and God kept drawing [Lewis] to Himself. And then he read Chesterton's Everlasting Man, and at that point he began to see that maybe Christianity was not so intellectually in the dark as he had thought. He was on this this journey, and what he is doing at this point was looking for reasons to not believe in the Christian faith. And yet without him even trying things are coming into his life that forced him to look at Christianity and see it is not such a open and shut case. And then one evening Tolkien and another friend Hugo Dyson invited Lewis to dine with them at Magdalen College. After dinner they started talking about myth, now this is something that Lewis had though about a great deal... and by myth he meant something false, not true. They discussed this all the way as they walked this wind blown Addison's walk. He always loved myth, but myth was not fact, it was something that was false; and that is the same category that he put Christianity in. But as Tolkien pushed him and Tolkien said "Jack don't you understand that these older myths, are glimpses that people had received of what was really going to happen. They went into Lewis's room and hammered away at it till 4 in the morning and at the end, Lewis believed. Because what Tolkien and Hugo Dyson had showed him is that at one point, however, myth became fact. Well, "bam", a light came on for him. And Lewis said "I never really thought about it like that before." What he began to realize is that myth is not false. Myth participates in truth. And so you have all of these different myth storylines and each reflect the truth. He (Lewis) recognizes that myth is the truth that has survived. And the reason that it has survived is that it appeals to the human imagination. And indeed the ancient myths of all cultures represented human imagination's attempts to express their understanding of the relationship between human beings and divine power. And of course that is the reason there are so many similarities in the myths of so many different cultures. All of these come out of this common origin, but what happens is that Christianity is the true myth. It hold on to everything that is true and it actually becomes historical fact; that is that this dying god that all of these other myths talk about actually happens in Christianity, you can date it." "The Magic Never Ends: The life and work of C.S. Lewis" Duncan Entertainment, 2003, Documentary, minutes 15:00-19:30

After some class presentations and an interview, I had a privileged lunch with Christopher Mitchel, a Lewis Scholar and the curator of the Wade Center at Wheaton College. We discussed the power of the legacy of Lewis and Tolkien and their groundbreaking works of fantasy literature. Tolkien is a self-proclaimed intentional myth-maker, and the Narnia stories have been called the most important pieces of children's mythic literature of the twentieth century. What we came to realize is that through their intentionality of choosing to write in the mythical fantasy genre, they were hoping to not only awaken the power of the human imagination, they were trying to get us back in touch with true reality which is more like a fantasy story then the modern nonfiction or even the modern fiction of their time. We both laughed at the tremendous irony that modern atheists and the like think that they are hurting Christianity by calling it legend, myth, or fantasy. We realized that Chesterton, Lewis, and Tolkien almost prophetically preemptively struck at that idea by leaning into the concept not away from it. When an atheist looks at a superman movie, or a harry potter movie, or the Narnia and Lord of the Rings movies and books noting the supernatural components embedded with the characters and then reads the gospels; one can see why they might conclude that Jesus as a character in a mythical story is like another wizard or superhero in another fantasy story or in a Hebrew myth. The beauty of this idea is that Jesus outdoes all of the main heroes in any fantasy story (combined). And one of the many things that Lewis and Tolkien and Chesterton wanted us to realize is that we are in the ultimate epic adventure super hero story ever being written. It all started "In the beginning..." and then in the book of Acts the church is born and we are all invited into this supernatural exciting adventure of Kingdom building here on Earth as it is in Heaven. The book of Acts has some amazing supernatural exciting adventurous mythical components to it. It is filled with power, miracles, signs, wonders - epic fantasy story stuff. And yet all of the supernatural components to the new testament are not just an awesome story; it is History. It is the true story. It is The True Fantasy Story: the ultimate oxymoron and a living breathing paradox. Christopher Mitchel famously said (with a big grin on his face) "The book of Acts does not have 'The End' in it. This is intentional; we are in that story and we are writing chapter 2,016..." This is the journey that we are in, invited into, and get to invite others into. The Fantasy stories that Chesterton, Tolkien, and Lewis wrote were meant to intentionally awaken us and point us to, not away from, the True Fantasy story, the True Myth, the True Epic – the one that we are in. This last unit (act) is about continuing or starting the process of waking up to this exciting way to see reality and your life. This unit (act) is an invitation to greater participation in this exciting supernatural adventure story that we are in!

Listen to and Ponder: "We are No longer a slave to fear we are children of God!" (Bethel Music: No Longer Slaves)

> 14 For all who are led by the Spirit of God are sons of God..15 For you did not receive the spirit of slavery to fall back into fear, but you have received the Spirit of adoption as sons, by whom we cry, "Abba! Father!"16 The Spirit himself bears witness with our spirit that we are children of God,17 and if children, then heirs-heirs of God and fellow heirs with Christ, provided we suffer with him in order that we may also be glorified with him. Romans 8:14-17

©2010, 2017. Wheaton Press™ All Rights Reserved.

The True Myth: "All Great Stories Point to the True Great Story"

The "Unfinished Story" ~ DISCUSSION NOTES:

God has made us free… set us free by his Grace and sealed us for the day of redemption.
This is the finished story. The Son has set you free. #GRACE. DONE.
CHAINS GONE. There is no divine manipulation, he is not co dependent, he will not punish or condemn… he is for you not against you. You and I are the Beloved Children of the King of the universe. God is our Father and Jesus is our Older Brother and His Holy Spirit is in us! This is the Mystery of the Gospel "Christ in us." Colossians 1:7

The Ending of Acts: Acts 28:30-31
30 He lived there two whole years at his own expense, and welcomed all who came to him,
31 proclaiming the kingdom of God and teaching about the Lord Jesus Christ with all boldness and without hindrance.

"THIS IS NOT THE END... IN SOME RESPECTS IT IS THE BEGINNING!"
ALL GREAT STORIES POINT TO THE TRUE STORY!
MANY OF US ARE NOT AWARE OF OR UTILIZING THE POWER WE ALREADY HAVE IN US!

DISCUSSION TOPIC: Jesus's Disciples & Superman's Disciples and the The TRUE SUPER HERO STORY: Pentecost!
We are invited to be Jesus' disciples - to be like him - to do what he did (not just know what he said or just to tell others about Him – which is good to do.) The full gospel message is not just that we have been saved for heaven - it is that we are free to experience heaven here and now not just later… that is why he taught his disciples, and therefore us, to pray "thy Kingdom come thy will be done on earth as it is in Heaven." Here and now. **Remember - Disciples don't just tell you about their teacher... They do what he did!** We are not just supposed to tell the world about what Jesus did and who he is... If he wanted us to do that he would have told us to do that in his great commission!

He said to go do it. Not just go talk about it – that what "go make Disciples" means – he could have said go and make believers but he said go and make Disciples – disciples are believers and doers. And he knew that it's not good news and it's not possible to do it without his power. So - When you became a Christian you were made new and you were filled with his spirit. It's called the indwelling of the Holy Spirit. (asking Jesus into your heart. He actually came in.)

This Gospel message would be cruel if Jesus did not give us the ability to do what he did (as his body manifested in a variety of gifts and abilities meant to work together. I Corinthians 12 & 13). Just like the avengers or the super heroes or the fellowship of the rings characters all have different gifts and special powers- so do you and I!

In order for us to have the ability to be like Him and do what He asked us to do He MUST give us the power and the mind and the love to be like He was and is in order to do what he did and is doing through us and in us.
AND THEN WE MUST LIVE, LOVE, THINK, AND BEHAVE LIKE HIM!

Pentecost begins with the giving power so that we can actually go be like Christ… otherwise if he said to be like him and did not give us the power to do so, he is cruel. Keep in mind that Satan's two big we   ut you and about God and use fear to keep you from doing the Kingdom work you

Who wants to bring in the Kingdom, here and now?
Who Wants to Kill dragons and reclaim Kingdom treasure.
Who Want to tear down strongholds, demolish arguments!
Who wants to crush the orphan spirit and the spirit of poverty?
Who wants to dismiss the religious Pharisee spirit?
Who wants to set captives free?
Who wants to proclaim the good news?
Who wants to Love?
You and I are Commissioned!

READ ISAIAH 61!

 ©2010, 2017. Wheaton Press™ All Rights Reserved.

The True Myth: "All Great Stories Point to the True Great Story"

The "Unfinished Story":

GERARD MANLEY HOPKINS:
As Kingfishers Catch Fire

As kingfishers catch fire, dragonflies draw flame;
As tumbled over rim in roundy wells
Stones ring; like each tucked string tells, each hung bell's
Bow swung finds tongue to fling out broad its name;
Each mortal thing does one thing and the same:
Deals out that being indoors each one dwells;
Selves — goes itself; myself it speaks and spells,
Crying Whát I dó is me: for that I came.

I say móre: the just man justices;
Keeps grace: thát keeps all his goings graces;
Acts in God's eye what in God's eye he is —
Chríst — for Christ plays in ten thousand places,
Lovely in limbs, and lovely in eyes not his
To the Father through the features of men's faces."

Photo Public Domain Yahoo Images

THE FINISHED STORY: Ephesians 4:30 "You are sealed for the day of redemption."

BECAUSE JESUS SAVED YOU and if you invited him into your life as lord as savior – THEN the spirit that raised Jesus from the dead - is in you!

THE UNFINSHED STORY: Romans 8:9-11 "9 But you are not controlled by your sinful nature. You are controlled by the Spirit if you have the Spirit of God living in you. (And remember that those who do not have the Spirit of Christ living in them do not belong to him at all.) 10 And Christ lives within you, so even though your body will die because of sin, the Spirit gives you life[d] because you have been made right with God. 11 The Spirit of God, who raised Jesus from the dead, lives in you. And just as God raised Christ Jesus from the dead, he will give life to your mortal bodies by this same Spirit living within you.

He is already in you. (If you do not readily believe this, you can take care of that today...there a many people who would love to guide you through that step of the journey. You could choose it right now...)

- This is the in-dwelling Holy Spirit! He sent it and we have that same Holy Spirit!
It is happening and this is another invitation it to have more of it happen...
An invitation to continue on or join in "The Unfinished story!"

VERSES TO UNPACK FOR THE JOURNEY:

Romans 8:14-17 – Children and Co-heirs with Christ...
John 14:12 – "Truly, truly, I say to you, whoever believes in me will also do the works that I do; and greater works than these will he do, because I am going to the Father."
Ephesians 4:30 - You are sealed for the day of redemption...
Romans 8:9-11 - The Spirit of God, who raised Jesus from the dead, lives in you...
Acts 1:12-15 – 120 people all together in one place, including Jesus' mom!
Acts 2:1-4 - Tongues of fire on each one of them...Filled with the Holy Spirit
Acts 2:38-39 - for you, your children, all who are far off, everyone who is called...
1 John 4:4 - He who is in you is greater than he who is in the world.
Matthew 28:18-19 - Go therefore and make disciples of all nations...
Matthew 9:17 – New Wineskins for new Wine...
Colossians 1:7 - Mystery of the gospel is Christ in you...
Romans 8 – All of it!
Acts 28:30-31 (End of Acts) "30 He lived there two whole years at his own expense, and welcomed all who came to him, 31 proclaiming the kingdom of God and teaching about the Lord Jesus Christ with all boldness and without hindrance.

©2010, 2017. Wheaton Press™ All Rights Reserved.   151

The True Myth: "All Great Stories Point to the True Great Story"

"[Much] of what passes for spirituality and spiritual practice--prayer days, meditation, retreats, spiritual direction, contemplation, ritual, and study--is primarily informed by an exclusive attention to the self and perhaps family relationships, suggesting that much of what we call spirituality is actually some mixture of psychology and private devotion, made sacred by the use of religious imagery. My argument is not that it's worthless, but that it's woefully incomplete. I am concerned that it provides a very limited experience of what Jesus is so passionate about, namely the "Reign of God" (the most repeated phrase in the four Gospels). As I understand the Reign of God, it includes the grace-driven, love-driven transformation of the self and the world. What's more, it recognizes that the transformation of the self and the world are directly connected to each other. . . .

Isn't it instructive that the spiritual formation of the original disciples happens with Jesus on the road? In effect, the disciples learn by doing. They grow into an understanding of this God of love, this God of compassion, this God who loves justice, this God who makes all things new, by participating as active observers and agents of compassion, justice, and newness. And, yes, necessarily, they pause with Jesus to reflect, ask questions (sometimes stupid questions), and pray. But the spiritual adventure described in the four Gospels does not happen in the sanctuary; it happens on the road, in the company of beggars, prostitutes, and lepers."
Richard Rhor

VERSES TO DISCUSS AND PONDER:

Acts 1:12-15: 13 And when they had entered, they went up to the upper room, where they were staying, Peter and John and James and Andrew, Philip and Thomas, Bartholomew and Matthew, James the son of Alphaeus and Simon the Zealot and Judas the son of James. 14 All these with one accord were devoting themselves to prayer, together with the women and Mary the mother of Jesus, and his brothers. 15 In those days Peter stood up among the brothers (the company of persons was in all about 120) and said…

Acts 2:1-4: 1 When the day of Pentecost arrived, they were all together in one place.
2 And suddenly there came from heaven a sound like a mighty rushing wind, and it filled the entire house where they were sitting.
3 And divided tongues as of fire appeared to them and rested on each one of them.
4 And they were all filled with the Holy Spirit....

Acts 2:38-39: 38 And Peter said to them, "Repent and be baptized every one of you in the name of Jesus Christ for the forgiveness of your sins, and you will receive the gift of the Holy Spirit. 39 For the promise is for you and for your children and for all who are far off, everyone whom the Lord our God calls to himself."

John 14:12 "Truly, truly, I say to you, whoever believes in me will also do the works that I do; and greater works than these will he do, because I am going to the Father.

1 John 4:4 Little children, you are from God and have overcome them, for he who is in you is greater than he who is in the world.

Matthew 28:18-19:18 And Jesus came and said to them, "All authority in heaven and on earth has been given to me. 19 Go therefore and make disciples…

Being saved is trusting Jesus to save you.
Being a disciple is acting like Jesus, loving like Jesus, and doing what Jesus did to bring his dominion here to earth!

"The Mystery of the gospel is Christ in you!"

We call this the indwelling of the Holy Spirit - the same spirit in Elijah, and David, and the Early Christian in the book of act is in us. It the Old Testament the Holy Spirit Came Upon Someone and into the Temple.

In the New - He comes INTO US AND DWELLS IN US. We are the New Temple!

 ©2010, 2017. Wheaton Press™ All Rights Reserved.

The True Myth: "All Great Stories Point to the True Great Story"

Insight into the World of Philosophy with *Lord of the Rings*

Trust: A primer on philosophy

THE TRUE MYTH! — ALL STORIES POINT US TO THE TRUE STORY...

Who would take a ring?

"All of them were deceived..."

Looking at the The four world views as "Rings of Power" and pieces of fractured reality...

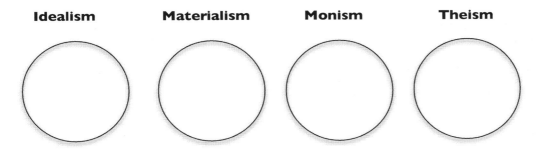

| Idealism | Materialism | Monism | Theism |

HISTORY BECAME LEGEND AND LEGEND BECAME MYTH"
(Min 5:30 of the extended version of the film.)

The ring: we need to destroy it before it destroys us.

You are The "Fellowship of the Ring"

Sam and Frodo On the Stairs Of Cirith Ungol in the Two Towers:

"I don't like anything here at all,' said Frodo, 'step or stone, breath or bone. Earth, air and water all seem accursed. But so our path is laid.'

'Yes, that's so,' said Sam. 'And we shouldn't be here at all, if we'd known more about it before we started. But I suppose it's often that way. The brave things in the old tales and songs, Mr. Frodo: adventures, as I used to call them. I used to think that they were things the wonderful folk of the stories went out and looked for, because they wanted them, because they were exciting and life was a bit dull, a kind of a sport, as you might say. But that's not the way of it with the tales that really mattered, or the ones that stay in the mind. Folk seem to have been just landed in them, usually – their paths were laid that way, as you put it. But I expect they had lots of chances, like us, of turning back, only they didn't. And if they had, we shouldn't know, because they'd have been forgotten. We hear about those as just went on – "and not all to a good end, mind you; at least not to what folk inside a story and not outside it call a good end. You know, coming home, and finding things all right, though not quite the same – like old Mr. Bilbo. But those aren't always the best tales to hear, though they may be the best tales to get landed in! I wonder what sort of a tale we've fallen into?'

'I wonder,' said Frodo. 'But I don't know. And that's the way of a real tale. Take any one that you're fond of. You may know, or guess, what kind of a tale it is, happy-ending or sad-ending, but the people in it don't know. And you don't want them to."

"No, sir, of course not. Beren now, he never thought he was going to get that Silmaril from the Iron Crown in Thangorodrim, and yet he did, and that was a worse place and a blacker danger than ours. But that's a long tale, of course, and goes on past the happiness and into grief and beyond it – and the Silmaril went on and came to Eärendil. And why, sir, I never thought of that before! We've got – you've got some of the light of it in that star-glass that the Lady gave you! Why, to think of it, we're in the same tale still! It's going on. Don't the great tales never end?'

'No, they never end as tales,' said Frodo. 'But the people in them come, and go when their part's ended. Our part will end later – or sooner.'

'And then we can have some rest and some sleep,' said Sam. He laughed grimly. 'And I mean just that, Mr. Frodo. I mean plain ordinary rest, and sleep, and waking up to a morning's work in the garden. I'm afraid that's all I'm hoping for all the time. "All the big important plans are not for my sort. Still, I wonder if we shall ever be put into songs or tales. We're in one, of course; but I mean: put into words, you know, told by the fireside, or read out of a great big book with red and black letters, years and years afterwards. And people will say: "Let's hear about Frodo and the Ring!" And they'll say: "Yes, that's one of my favourite stories. Frodo was very brave, wasn't he, dad?" "Yes, my boy, the famousest of the hobbits, and that's saying a lot.""

"It's saying a lot too much,' said Frodo, and he laughed, a long clear laugh from his heart. Such a sound had not been heard in those places since Sauron came to Middle-earth. To Sam suddenly it seemed as if all the stones were listening and the tall rocks leaning over them. But Frodo did not heed them; he laughed again. 'Why, Sam,' he said, 'to hear you somehow makes me as merry as if the story was already written. But you've left out one of the chief characters: Samwise the stouthearted. "I want to hear more about Sam, dad. Why didn't they put in more of his talk, dad? That's what I like, it makes me laugh. And Frodo wouldn't have got far without Sam, would he, dad?"'

'Now, Mr. Frodo,' said Sam, 'you shouldn't make fun. I was serious.'

'So was I,' said Frodo, 'and so I am. We're going on a bit too fast. You and I, Sam, are still stuck in the worst places of the story, and it is all too likely that some will say at this point: "Shut the book now, dad; we don't want to read any more.""

"Maybe,' said Sam, 'but I wouldn't be one to say that. Things done and over and made into part of the great tales are different. Why, even Gollum might be good in a tale, better than he is to have by you, anyway. And he used to like tales himself once, by his own account. I wonder if he thinks he's the hero or the villain?

'Gollum!' he called. 'Would you like to be the hero - now where's he got to again?'

J.R.R. Tolkien, Two Towers Book 4 Ch. 8

 ©2010, 2017. Wheaton Press™ All Rights Reserved.

The True Myth: Notes on myth to contemplate and discuss
"All Great Myths Point Us to the True Myth"

Lewis's definition of myth

"Lewis believed in a prime reality. That prime reality is the Eternal God. Myth is man's way of understanding the prime reality, and also is a deep call from that prime reality drawing man upwards toward it. C.S. Lewis's concept of man holds that there are two basic characteristics, or needs of man: the need to know and the need to worship. Man knows things through rational thought or the making of statements, but these systems of rational thought and statements destroy the object they are describing. Man intellectualizes in order to know, but in doing this destroys the object. Thus man has a third need: that of imagination. Imagination becomes the means by which man explains or describes the prime reality. Man needs imaginative thought because man is more than rational thought. Lewis believes that reality is larger than rationality. Carl Jung believes that there are three basic parts to an archetype: the personal unconscious, unconscious, and the collective unconscious. This collective unconscious is a racial history embedding in man from even before his birth, and from this history arises primordial images, passed down through past events. These primordial images are used by poets to create a feeling of deep emotion. This emotion is possible because of the racial history embedded in every man. Poets (via literature) are the only ones able to capture these primordial images and evoke this essential story-feeling in the reader." (Sammie Quarterman)

C.S. Lewis's meaning of myth

"Lewis was writing brilliantly imagined and exacting 'science fiction' long before the term was current, and using it, as he used children's fiction, to convey a deep conviction about God and about living with a subtlety and symbolic power perhaps to be found elsewhere only in the work of his beloved Edmund Spencer." (London Times)

We need to define what Lewis meant by myth in order to understand his fiction.
- Believes myth is written in all periods, even modern ones
- Myth is a thing, not a narration
- Myth may not possess any narrative element
- A great myth contains universal truth
- Myth is always awe-inspiring and numinous (holy)
- Unlike lesser literature in which the reader follows a plot to its logical conclusion and then puts the book aside, in myth he is likely to feel a new world of meaning taking permanent root in him
- Myth also is concerned always with the:
  - Impossible
  - Preternatural (existing outside of nature)
  - Serious and grave

- ### What is the cause of myth-making?
  - There is a great, sovereign, uncreated, unconditional reality "at the core of things"
  - Myth is on the one hand a kind of picture—making what helps man to understand this reality—and on the other hand the result of a deep call from that reality
  - Myth is "a real though unfocused gleam of divine truth falling on human imagination" which enables man to express the inexpressible

©2010, 2017. Wheaton Press™ All Rights Reserved.

The True Myth: "All Great Stories Point to the True Great Story"
Tolkien and the Mythic Epic Adventure

Quotes on Myth for Class Discussion

With a highlighter, highlight three quotes that resonate to you.

1) "Myth, we may say, is the transmissions of the cumulative knowledge, experiences, and universal truths constant in our human existence, through the consistent symbologies known to folklore." (Joseph Cambel)

2) "The common element that bound the presentations together was the conviction that in the day when many are calling for 'demythologizing' of Christianity. More attention should be paid to creative literatures who have offered a more healthy alternative: the use of literary myth to clarify and reinforce the creedial heart of the Christian message." (Clyde S. Kilby)

3) "We need joy. The birth of Christ is the eucatastrophe of man's history. The resurrection is the eucatastrophe of the story of the incarnation. This story begins and ends in joy! There is no tale ever told that men would rather find as true, and none which so many skeptical men have accepted as true on its own merits." (J.R.R. Tolkien)

4) "I am a Christian, and of course what I write will be from that essential viewpoint." (J.R.R. Tolkien)

5) "Once he showed me an unpublished paper by a British professor. The idea of which was that *The Lord of the Rings* is misunderstood by critics because they failed to see that it is based on the manner of Christ's redemption of the world. To this Tolkien said 'Much of this is true enough—except of course, the general impression given—that I had any such 'schema' in my conscious mind before or during writing it.' It was against this ticketed didacticism that Tolkien found it necessary to make his disclaimer. I think he was afraid that the allegorical dragon might gobble up the art and the myth." (Clyde S. Kilby)

6) "Gustave Alulie has demonstrated the centrality of the Christus Vi Clor Motif in the entire New Testament Message: Jesus born of a woman is in fact the divine Christ who conquers the evil power that brought the race into bondage and thereby restores mankind! From such universal and therefore impressively objective archetypal motifs can the Christian literature draw his themes and patterns thereby creating stores that, if artistically and seriously executed, are sure to strike the deep reaches of man's being and point him toward the Christ who fulfilled the myths and legends of the world." (John W. Montgomery)

7) "The myth became flesh. This is not a religion nor a philosophy; it's the summing up and actuality of them all. For this is the marriage of heaven and earth: perfect Myth and perfect Fact; claiming not only our love and obedience but also our wonder and delight." (C.S. Lewis)

8) "We see, though not with the eye." (William Blake)

9) "Enchanted trees give all ordinary trees a measure of enchantment." (J.W. Montgomery)

10) "I believe in Christianity as I believe that the sun has risen: not only because I see it, but because by it I see everything else." (C.S. Lewis.)

The True Myth: "All Great Stories Point to the True Great Story"

Quotes on Myth for Class Discussion
With a highlighter, highlight three quotes that resonate to you.

11) "Frodo asked, 'Why was I chosen?' Gandalf replied. 'You may be sure that it was not for any merit that others do not possess: not for power or wisdom at any rate. But you have been chosen, and you must therefore use such strength and heart and wits as you have." (J.R.R. Tolkien)

12) "Tolkien believes that at certain moments fantasy can so affect the spirit that it is put suddenly in touch with a deeper reality." (Randel Helms)

13) "Myth is necessary because reality is so much larger than rationality. Not that myth is irrational, but that it accommodates the rational while rising above it." (Clyde S. Kilby)

14) "Man is fundamentally mythic. His real health depends upon his knowing and living in metaphysical totality." (Clyde S. Kilby)

15) "A friend once asked William Blake, 'When the sun rises, do you not see a round disk of fire, something like a guinea?' To which he replied, 'Oh no, I see an immeasurable company of the heavenly hosts crying, 'Holy holy is the Lord God Almighty.'" (Clyde S. Kilby)

16) "In the center of Tolkien's consciousness is Middle Earth, yet its inner consistency and universal values of courage, hope, endurance, and compassion touch each of us in our centers of being, hopefully stimulating our creative imaginations in the myth building process. Thus, a reading of Tolkien's trilogy is an experience rather than an intellectual exercise." (Anne C. Petty)

17) "There is no didactic prescription of the right way to live. In other words, instead of moralizing about the corruptness of men and their damnation through their sins, demanding that one must be good and turn the other cheek in the face of adversity, Tolkien has Frodo show compassion for the miserable Gollum... and we believe it. The temptation and fall of Boromir is more eloquent than many sermons, and we listen to it." (Anne C. Petty)

18) "Tolkien once told a friend that he was distressed that the English had so few myths of their own and had to live on foreign borrowings, 'So I thought I'd make myself one!'" (Randel Helms)

19) "Moving from the central to the particular, *The Lord of the Rings* illustrates the satisfactory completion of the myth as a means through which man may confront the ultimate truths of his universe, achieving a sense of integration from that confrontation." (Joseph Cambel)

20) "The poetry of mythic imagination will not, for Tolkien, replace religion so much as make it possible, putting imaginatively starved modern man back once again into awed and reverent contact with a living universe." (Randel Helms)

©2010, 2017. Wheaton Press™ All Rights Reserved.

The True Myth: Notes on myth to contemplate and discuss
"All Great Myths Point Us to the True Myth"

C.S. Lewis on Myth: "The glory of the morning star is somehow not enough glory for us. We deeply desire more, and it is at this point that poetry and mythology come to our aid."

Lewis says, "We do not want merely to see beauty… We want something else which can hardly be put into words—to be united with the beauty we see, to pass into it, to receive it into ourselves, to bath in it, to become part of it. (That is one reason why we have coupled air and earth and water with gods and goddesses and nymphs and elves)."

Myth Class Discussion Notes:

We see, though not with the eye.

William Blake

Artwork courtesy of Prince Tim Burchfield

 ©2010, 2017. Wheaton Press™ All Rights Reserved.

The True Myth: "All Great Stories Point to the True Great Story"

Tolkien and the Mythic Epic Adventure: "APPLICABILITY"
The Lord of the Rings and Myth

Foreword to the Second Edition by Tolkien

"The real war does not resemble the legendary war in its process or its conclusion. If it had inspired or directed the development of the legend, then certainly the Ring would have been seized and used against Sauron; he would not have been annihilated but enslaved, and Barad would not have been destroyed but occupied. Saruman, failing to get possession of the Ring, would in the confusion and treacheries of the time have found in Mordor the missing links in his own researches into Ring-lore, and before long he would have made a Great Ring of his own with which to challenge the self-styled Ruler of Middle Earth. In that conflict both sides would have held hobbits in hatred and contempt: they would not long have survived even as slaves.

"Other arrangements could be devised according to the tastes or views of those who like allegory or topical reference. But I cordially dislike allegory in all its manifestations, and always have done so since I grew old and wary enough to detect its presence. I much prefer history, true or feigned, with its varied applicability to the thought and experience of the readers. I think that many confuse 'applicability' with 'allegory'; but the one resides in the freedom of the reader, and the other in the purposed domination of the author."

Applicability Notes

I am a
Christian
and
of course
what I write
will be
from that
essential
viewpoint

J.R.R. Tolkien

Artwork courtesy of Prince Tim Burchfield

MYTH & Practicing Applicability: *The Silmarillion*

Notes on *The Silmarillion,*

Ainundale: The music of the Ainur

Imagination, love, wonder, and joy (Genesis 1)
God is powerful and in control—appreciate creation

Take notes on:

1) The Ainur (pg. 15) and the Valar (pg. 20)

1) Melkor (pg. 16)

1) Ulmo (pg. 19)

1) Manwe (pg. 19)

1) Aule (pg. 19)

1) Ea (pg. 20, 25)

1) The Children of Iluvitar (pg. 20)

Write a paragraph of personal Reader Response to Ainundale.

Valenquenta

Take notes on:

1) The Secret Fire (pg. 25)

1) Of the Valar (explain the connection you have with one that you identify with)
      - Read I Corinthians 12 and 13

1) Elbereth (pg. 26)

1) Of the Enemies (pg. 31-32)

1) Melkor (pg. 31)

2) Valaraukar (pg. 31)

1) Sauron (pg. 32)

Write a paragraph of personal Reader Response to Valequenta.

 ©2010, 2017. Wheaton Press™ All Rights Reserved.

MYTH & Practicing Applicability: *The Silmarillion*
Notes on *The Silmarillion,* Part 2

The Silmarillion: Reading Mythically
More Notes on The Silmarillion For Class Discussion

1) How doe this "mythical story" point us to the True Story found in Genesis?

1) Extend your learning: Look up, read aloud in small groups, and discuss several other "Creation Stories" form religions all over the world, past and present.

2) In the Story Melkor is a fallen angelic type of being – what was his "sin"? Furthermore, in his rebellion, he does not fight against the God character, Melkor fights with the other angels and with the created beings. What can this teach us about Satan's position and limited power for our Story, particularly considering some key verses in several chapters of Ephesians, especially Ch. 6.

3) Melkor wants to ruin the creation but is unable to because the All-Powerful Creator God in the story redeems and weaves all of his attempts into the pattern of the full story. If you were Melkor, how would this make you feel. What are the implications for us in our story when Satan tries to ruin God's plans…

Scripture Reading Integrity Assignments
MYTH & Practicing Applicability:
1 Corinthians and *The Silmarillion*

Read and annotate the first letter to the church at Corinth written by the Apostle Paul as a letter in one sitting. Pretend you are a member of the church. Where do you see connections to our discussion on Myth and *The Silmarillion?* The connections you make can be subtle, overt, literary, historical, artistic, personal, or metaphoric.

In the space below, write down at least three verses that you find engaging, and briefly explain why you picked these verses. Cut and paste or write out the entire verse, but do not simply put the reference. Do not summarize the verse as a response.

    ©2010, 2017. Wheaton Press™ All Rights Reserved.

MYTH & Practicing Applicability: *The Hobbit* An Unexpected Adventure!
All great myths point us to the true myth

Mythical connections with THE HOBBIT
Look at the introduction to the first movie "The Hobbit: An Unexpected Journey"

"The MONSTERS AND THE CRITICS" Monsters Reveal and Attack our weaknesses!"
- Bilbo goes on an adventure to kill a dragon and reclaim treasure… How can we do this in our own lives?

The Invitation to go on an adventure! Don't Miss it!

Artwork courtesy of Prince Elijah Age 7

MYTH & Practicing Applicability: *The Hobbit:* "Riddles in the Dark"
"Riddles in the Dark"

As you read an annotate, identify and label the following literary tools for applicability:

1) Symbols

2) Metaphors & Similes

2) Overarching Metaphors

3) Paradoxes

4) Myth/ Mythical Elements - applicability

5) Biblical Allusions (with references)

Write down some of your favorite riddles for our class discussion.

> *"Voiceless it cries,*
> *Wingless flutters,*
> *Toothless bites,*
> *Mouthless mutters."*
> Gullum in the Hobbit p. 81

Below, create your own riddle for the class.

Notes on "Riddles in the Dark" particularly on Jesus's "riddles" and how paradox can help us unlock riddles for us in the darkness we are wrapped in. We too do not want to get devoured by the one in our story that is prowling around in the dark... *(I Peter 5:8)*

Additional space for notes on "Riddles in the Dark":

Artwork courtesy of Princess Anna Age 7

 ©2010, 2017. Wheaton Press™ All Rights Reserved.

MYTH & Practicing Applicability: *The Hobbit:* "Riddles in the Dark"
All great myths point us to the true myth

Mythical connections with "Riddles in the Dark"

> *"Alive without breath,*
> *As cold as death;*
> *Never thirsty, ever drinking,*
> *All in mail never clinking."*
> Gullum in the Hobbit p. 83

WHY RIDDLES? What does it take to answer riddles?

> *"A box without hinges, key, or lid,*
> *Yet golden treasure inside is hid,"*
> Bilbo in the Hobbit p. 83

In Matthew 13:10, we're told that the disciples came to Jesus and said to him, "Why do you speak to them [the crowds who came to see Jesus] in parables?"

"To you it has been given to know the secrets of the kingdom of heaven, but to them it has not been given. For to the one who has, more will be given, and he will have an abundance, but from the one who has not, even what he has will be taken away. This is why I speak to them in parables, because seeing they do not see, and hearing they do not hear, nor do they understand. Indeed, in their case the prophecy of Isaiah is fulfilled that says:
"You will indeed hear but never understand, and you will indeed see but never perceive. For this people's heart has grown dull, and with their ears they can barely hear, and their eyes they have closed, lest they should see with their eyes and hear with their ears and understand with their heart and turn, and I would heal them."
But blessed are your eyes, for they see, and your ears, for they hear. For truly, I say to you, many prophets and righteous people longed to see what you see, and did not see it, and to hear what you hear, and did not hear it.

(Matt. 13:11-17)

©2010, 2017. Wheaton Press™ All Rights Reserved.

Scripture Reading Integrity Assignments
MYTH & Practicing Applicability: *The Hobbit*: "Riddles in the Dark"
Colossians and *The Hobbit*: "Riddles in the Dark"

Read and annotate the letter to the church of Colossae written by the Apostle Paul as a letter in one sitting. Pretend you are a member of the church. Where do you see connections to our discussion on Tolkien's *The Hobbit*? The connections you make can be subtle, overt, literary, historical, artistic, personal, or metaphoric.

In the space below, write down at least three verses that you find engaging, and briefly explain why you picked these verses. Cut and paste or write out the entire verse, but do not simply put the reference. Do not summarize the verse as a response.

John Donne: "Death be not proud"

DEATH be not proud, though some have called thee
Mighty and dreadfull, for, thou art not so,
For, those, whom thou think'st, thou dost overthrow,
Die not, poore death, nor yet canst thou kill me.
From rest and sleepe, which but thy pictures bee,
Much pleasure, then from thee, much more must flow,
And soonest our best men with thee doe goe,
Rest of their bones, and soules deliverie.
Thou art slave to Fate, Chance, kings, and desperate men,
And dost with poyson, warre, and sicknesse dwell,
And poppie, or charmes can make us sleepe as well,
And better then thy stroake; why swell'st thou then;

One short sleepe past, wee wake eternally,
And death shall be no more, death thou shalt die.

©2010, 2017. Wheaton Press™ All Rights Reserved.

The True Myth: A Final Lesson – Life as Epic Adventure and Journey

In this workbook I use Tolkien's Lord of the Rings as a model to talk about spiritual journey, or what some people call spiritual formation. In the next few pages you will be tracking and describing key scenes with excellent metaphors from Frodo's Journey. Then the assignment is to learn from Tolkien's Epic adventure and apply lessons from his Story to your own personal epic adventure Story. Like I have said – great stories point to the True Great Story; the one that we are in!

Of course you do not have to use Tolkien's epic, there are several good choices! The goal is to use the key metaphors in the story to guide you in learning about your own journey. Rarely are the metaphors in the same order or on the same scale – but if you will put the effort, creativity, and openness into the task at hand you will be amazed at how well these stories point to and teach us about your own journey and adventure.

For the Final Exam you should pick a story and find 12 scenes for metaphoric application. Preferably these scenes should be split between positive and negative aspects of the journey. Chart the scenes from the tale you choose to follow and then make a "METAPHOR MAP" for your own story showing the parallels, truths, and lessons to take with you on your own journey.

If you do not want to use Tolkien's epic simply find one of your favorites and use my template or Propps Dramatis Personae to guide you on your hunt for metaphors. Probably the easier alternative that fit's the allegorical, mythical model is something like Hinds Feet on High Places or Pilgrim's Progress. I chose Lord of the Rings because it goes along with the
Inklings theme and style of literature.

Some Great Options:
The "Examine Packet" at the beginning of this Book.
Pilgrims Progress
Hinds Feet on High Places
The "12 Steps"
St John of the Cross: The Dark Night of the Soul
The Hobbit
C. S. Lewis: The Voyage of the Dawn Treaded or The Horse and His Boy
Star Wars
Batman, Superman, Spiderman etc…
Harry Potter
Homer's: The Odyssey
Beowulf
The Story of Moses, Joseph, Elijah, King David, St. Peter, St. Paul
Charles Dickens': Christmas Carol, Great Expectations
Jane Austin – Pride and Prejudice, Emma, Sense and Sensibility
Many of the Disney Movies work Great
Gladiator
A famous explorer… Shackleton
A famous musician, artist, athlete!
A famous leader, Lincoln, etc..
A famous builder, designer, inventor, scientist etc…
Any of Shakespeare's Plays: Hamlet, Midsummer Nights Dream, The Tempest
A well lived and loved Saint!

Some Metaphor Moments:
- Leaving
- Wounding
- Awakening
- Healing
- Calling
- Chosen
- Tempted
- Death and Resurrection
- Encounter
- Vision
- The Underworld
- The Wilderness
- Thriving and growth in trials
- Battle
- Loss
- Victory
- Training
- Fear
- Gifting

The True Myth: A Final Lesson – Life as Epic Adventure and Journey

This was the thought process I used to create the metaphor map from The Fellowship of the Ring. I took a few of the definitions of Propps morphology of the folk tale and placed them here to give an example of the process. This helps us analyze the concept that all stories have pieces of the archetypal MYTH or STORY. The Lord of the Rings is no exception. Look at the parallels found in fellowship of the Ring. Remember that one of the main goals of this final Act is to show that we are all on a Journey. That we are IN the Great Story being written by the Great Author. We are in the Story of the Book of Acts. But even more so we are all on our own personal journey. By Looking at the Great Myths, we can learn about our own story, and look for the hand of the author in our journey.

All great stories, legends, myths, movies, and novels have some of these, or all of these, or more, or different ones. The Key is that we can learn from other stories about our own story. No two stories or characters are alike or on the same adventure or have the exact same functions or actions. But there is much similarity. And much to learn through the power of metaphor and applicability.

USE THE SPACE BELOW TO BRAINSTORM IDEAS FOR YOUR NOVEL, MOVIE, MUSICAL, EPIC...

 ©2010, 2017. Wheaton Press™ All Rights Reserved.

Myth: A Final Lesson – Life as Epic Adventure and Journey

The Morphology of the Folktale
Appendix B
Propp's Functions of Dramatis Personae

The following is a simplified listing of Propp's functions of dramatis personae as described in his <u>Morphology of the Folktale</u> (1968, p. 25-65).

For each <u>function</u> of the dramatic personae in the folktale there is given:

　　　1) A brief summary of its "essence" as Propp called it, plus
　　　2) An abbreviated Definition of the function in one word.

- One of the members of a family absents himself from home**.** **Definition**: absentation.
- An interdiction (prohibition) is addressed to the hero. **Definition:** interdiction
- The interdiction is violated. **Definition:** violation
- The villain makes an attempt to reconnaissance**.** **Definition:** reconnaissance
- The villain receives information about his victim. **Definition:** delivery
- The villain attempts to deceive his victim in order to take possession of him or his belongings.
- **Definition:** trickery
- The victim submits to deception and thereby unwittingly helps his enemy. **Definition:** complicity
- The villain causes harm or injury to a member of a family. **Definition:** villainy
- One member of a family either lacks something or desires to have something. **Definition:** lack
- Misfortune or lack is made known; the hero is approached with a request or command; he is allowed to go or he is dispatched. **Definition**: mediation, the connective incident
- The seeker agrees to or decides upon counteraction. **Definition**: beginning counteraction
- The hero leaves home. **Definition**: departure
- The hero is tested, interrogated, attacked, etc., which prepares the way for his receiving either a magical agent or helper. **Definition**: the first function of the donor
- The hero reacts to the actions of the future donor. **Definition:** the hero's reaction
- The hero acquires the use of a magical agent. **Definition:** provision or receipt of a magical agent
- The hero is transferred, delivered, or led to the whereabouts of an object of search. Definition: spatial transference between two kingdoms, guidance
- The hero and the villain join in direct combat. **Definition:** struggle
- The hero returns. **Definition**: branding, marking
- The villain is defeated. **Definition:** victory
- The initial misfortune or lack is liquidated. **Definition:** liquidation
- The hero returns. **Definition:** return
- The hero is pursued. **Definition**: pursuit, chase
- Rescue of the hero from pursuit. **Definition**: rescue
- The hero, unrecognized, arrives home or in another country. **Definition**: unrecognized arrival
- A false hero presents unfounded claims. **Definition:** unfounded claims
- A difficult task is proposed to the hero. **Definition:** difficult task
- The task is resolved. Def**i**nition: solution
- The hero is recognized. **Definition:** recognition
- The false hero or villain is exposed. **Definition:** exposure
- The hero is given a new appearance. **Definition:** transfiguration
- The villain is punished. **Definition**: punishment
- The hero is married and ascends the throne. **Definition:** wedding

©2010, 2017. Wheaton Press™ All Rights Reserved.

Myth: A Final Lesson – Life as Epic Adventure and Journey
"The Quest": METAPHOR MAP)

"Frodo asked, 'Why was I chosen?' Gandalf replied. 'You may be sure that it was not for any merit that others do not possess: not for power or wisdom at any rate. But you have been chosen, and you must therefore use such strength and heart and wits as you have.'"

1) For the epic story you have selected, choose at least 12 events and describe aspects of this moment of the Journey below - remember the more details you use in your descriptions the better opportunity you have for the metaphors later...

- ❑ You must include at least 4 "Encouraging moments"
- ❑ You must include at least 4 "Challenging moments"

2) On this sheet jot down some or all of the following in the space provided to help with the metaphor and applicability for the "My Quest" Pages.

Put *At least three (3) of the following down for each spot...*
- ✓ **Significance of the Location – Actions and Characters**
- ✓ **Interaction with Friends or Foes/Monsters** *("Monsters reveal and attach our weaknesses." Tolkien)*
- ✓ **Lessons learned during this segment of the Quest**
- ✓ **Gifts received, wounds, losses, victories, & defeats**

3) More fun just for fun: chart your Hero's journey on a map of the story...

TITLE OF Book, Musical, or Movie: ___Interstellar___

#1: ___Cooper, Tom and Murph accidentally meet Airdrone and take it down
- In the beginning of movie. A air drone flew by Cooper and kinda on the way school. After a adventurous ride.
- Cooper hacked it and took it down
- daughter Murph asked can we let him go. Cooper answer. "The thing need to learn how to adapt, like rest of us"

#2: ___After dust storm, Cooper and Murph found the strange gravity change
- The dust
-
-

#3: _____:
-
-
-

#4: _____
-
-
-

NOTE: *ON THE DAY OF THE FINAL, please come prepared discuss your response to how your quest fits into the content of this semester. You will be taking the Philosophy Grid Quiz again and then briefly sharing on the "Aslan Moment Encounter Lesson" and this "Quest" Lesson.*

Myth: A Final Lesson – Life as Epic Adventure and Journey
"The Quest": METAPHOR MAP)

#5: _____

-

-

-

#6: _____

-

-

-

#7: _____

-

-

-

#8: _____

-

-

-

#9: _____

-

-

-

#10: _____

-

-

-

#11: _____

-

-

-

#12: _____

-

-

-

Myth: A Final Lesson – Life as Epic Adventure and Journey
"My Quest": METAPHOR MAP

"Frodo asked, 'Why was I chosen?' Gandalf replied. 'You may be sure that it was not for any merit that others do not possess: not for power or wisdom at any rate. But you have been chosen, and you must therefore use such strength and heart and wits as you have.'"

1) Make a transfer application from Journey in **"The Quest"** to your personal Journey. Be creative! You may want to project and plan ahead for the future... or you can work from the past or present.

2) On this sheet jot down some or all of the following in the space provided to help with the metaphor and applicability for the "My Quest" Pages.

        Put *At least three (3) of the following down for each spot...*
- ✓ **Significance of the Location – Actions and Characters**
- ✓ **Interaction with Friends or Foes/Monsters** *("Monsters reveal and attach our weaknesses." Tolkien)*
- ✓ **Lessons learned during this segment of the Quest**
- ✓ **Gifts received, wounds, losses, victories, & defeats**

3) Create your own map (on an 8.5 X 11 sheet of paper), label each event with the transfer name, and trace your Journey on your personal map. You do not have to match the order of events in "The Quest" assignment...

TITLE OF Your Story! *(Your "Book, Musical, or Movie")*: _____

#1:_____: Can be like = _____

    In these ways:

#2:_____: Can be like = _____

    In these ways:

#3:_____: Can be like = _____

    In these ways:

#4:_____: Can be like = _____

    In these ways:

 ©2010, 2017. Wheaton Press™ All Rights Reserved.

Myth: A Final Lesson – Life as Epic Adventure and Journey
"MY Quest": METAPHOR MAP

#5:_____: Can be like = _____

In these ways:

#6:_____: Can be like = _____

In these ways:

#7:_____: Can be like = _____

In these ways:

#8:_____: Can be like = _____

In these ways:

#9:_____: Can be like = _____

In these ways:

#10:_____: Can be like = _____

In these ways:

#11:_____: Can be like = _____

In these ways:

#12:_____: Can be like = _____

In these ways:

©2010, 2017. Wheaton Press™ All Rights Reserved. 173

Philosophy & Theology

Myth: A Final Lesson – Life as Epic Adventure and Journey
The Fellowship of the Ring: "The Quest"
(AN EXAMPLE OF THE METAPHOR MAP)

"Frodo asked, 'Why was I chosen?' Gandalf replied. 'You may be sure that it was not for any merit that others do not possess: not for power or wisdom at any rate. But you have been chosen, and you must therefore use such strength and heart and wits as you have.'"

1) Locate each event and trace the journey on your group's map
2) On a poster board, PowerPoint or a prezzi, unlock metaphoric potential by writing down some or all of the following for each metaphoric moment, at least three per spot:
    - Significance of the location: actions and characters
    - Interaction with friends or foes/monsters
        ("Monsters Reveal and attack our weaknesses." J.R.R. Tolkien)
    - Lessons learned during this segment of the Quest
    - Gifts received, wounds, losses, victories, and defeats

1) Bag End in Hobbiton: *The Place and People to Fight FOR! ~ Inheriting Evil which needs to be destroyed before it destroys the hero and the community ~ The confession of the quest and the burden & the commitment of the friends to help ~ Realizing who are friends and foes ~ help from unexpected places*

2) Old Forest (Old Man Willow): Bickering ~ Lost the trail ~ Fatigue ~ *Unexpected attack ~ Call for Help ~ Unexpected Rescue*

3) Tom and Goldberry Bombadil's House: *Good is MORE powerful then Evil ~ Rest, Perspective, Context the Big Story that the hero finds himself in.*

4) The Barrow Downs and the Barrow-wights: *Spiritual Attack "buried alive" ~ Rescue, "Resurrection", Restoration, Equipped with armor, treasure, hope.*

5) Bree ("The Prancing Pony"): *Not the Shire ~ Change of plans, Gandalf does not show up ~ Made a mistake that was almost fatal ~ The King Joins the Journey ~ Almost killed by the Nazgul ~ Saved by the King ~ Learn about the enemy*

6) Weathertop (The Black Riders): *Friends make a mistake Frodo gets wounded, Frodo makes a mistake and he gets wounded, Aragorn is gone and Frodo gets wounded ~ Uses Fire and Sword to fight the darkness ~ using evil means to fight evil only makes it worse ~ if this wound is not cared for it will remove him from the Quest.*

7) The Ford at Rivendell: *We need to run from evil when it pursues us (I.E. Joseph) ~ We need to turn and Face the enemy from a safe place, Identity, Stand Firm, Resist evil ~ Friends help ~ Glorfindel lends him his horse ~ Enemy is washed away.*

8) Rivendell: *House of healing, worship, council, wisdom, rest, gifts (Mithril chain mail shirt & sword Sting) ~ joins the Fellowship and the Quest ~ Chooses to take the burden of the Ring*

9) Caradhras: Failed *attempt ~ Need to re-route ~ "People over Peak" there are other options besides sacrificing group members for the sake of the quest ~ Frodo has to make a hard decision between two bad options*

10) Moria (The Bridge of Khazad-dum): *Journey into the underworld, "the dark night" ~ hard decisions in the dark ~ "Treasures of Darkness", wisdom in the darkness ~ Battles in the darkness and under the surface ~ Gandalf fights the Balrag ~ Gandalf is taken off of the quest sacrificial death.*

11) Lothlorien ("Caras Galadhon"): *Place of rest, healing, morning, remembrance, strategy ~ Gimli misjudges Galadriel ~ Galadriel is tested ~ Frodo sees what will happen if he fails ~ a place of encouragement ~ powerful gifts, including racial reconciliation, dignity, honor, boats, weapons, food, clothing, friendship*

12) Sarn Gebir and Parth Galen (The Breaking of the Fellowship): *The group breaks up ~ Borimir is tempted and falls ~ Attack from within the group ~ The Kings lets Frodo Go and trusts him with the ring ~ Borimir shows that he is sorry and sacrifices his life for Merry and Pippin bestowing value on them and sending them and the enemy in the opposite direction of Frodo ~ Frodo and Sam head off together, Frodo cannot go alone ~ The Three friends chase after their friends who are captured*

 ©2010, 2017. Wheaton Press™ All Rights Reserved.

Myth: A Final Lesson – Life as Epic Adventure and Journey
The Fellowship of the Ring: "My Quest"
(AN EXAMPLE OF THE METAPHOR MAP)

a) On a poster board, PowerPoint, or prezzi: make a transfer application from the Fellowship's journey to your personal journey. Be creative! In your quest you may want to project and plan ahead from the future, or you can work from the past or present.

b) Be Sure to write down some or all of the following (at least three per stop on the quest)
  - Significance of the location, actions, and characters
  - Interaction with friends or foes/monsters
  - Lessons learned during this segment of the quest
  - Gifts received, wounds, losses, victories, and defeats

  c) Create your own map on an 8.5 X 11 sheet of paper, labeling each event with the transfer name and tracing your journey on your personal map. You do not have to match the Fellowship's order of events.

The Fellowship of

1) Bag End in Hobbiton: can be like
In these ways:

2) The Old Forest (Old Man Willow): can be like _____
In these ways:

3) Tom and Goldberry Bombadil's House: can be like
In these ways:

4) The Barrow Downs and the Barrow-wights: can be like
In these ways:

5) Bree ("The Prancing Pony"): can be like
In these ways:

6) Weathertop (The Black Riders): can be like
In these ways:

7) The Ford at Rivendell: can be like
In these ways:

8) Rivendell: can be like
In these ways:

9) Caradhras: can be like
In these ways:

10) Moria (The Bridge of Khazad-dum): can be like
In these ways:

11) Lothlorien ("Caras Galadhon"): can be like
In these ways:

12) Sarn Gebir and Parth Galen: can be like
In these ways:

©2010, 2017. Wheaton Press™ All Rights Reserved.

Tolkien and the Mythic Epic Adventure
The Adventure Myth

"The Road goes ever on and on down from the door where it began. Now far ahead the Road has gone, and I must follow, if I can, pursuing it with weary feet, until it joins some larger way, where many paths and errands meet. And whither then? I cannot say." (Frodo, *The Fellowship of the Ring,* Chapter 3)

"You shall go out with joy and be led forth in peace; the mountains and the hills will burst into song before you, and all the trees of the field will clap their hands!" (Isaiah 55:12)

The Magnet Project (take home assignment)

Find a quote from your story to creatively and attractively attach to a magnet.

Be prepared to explain to the class the following:
- Where it came from
- The context of the quote
- Why you chose it
- What it means to you personally and spiritually

Artwork Princess Micah Trautwein

 ©2010, 2017. Wheaton Press™ All Rights Reserved.

Myth: A Final Lesson — the Ultimate Goal of the Quest!

"Frodo asked, 'Why was I chosen?' Gandalf replied. 'You may be sure that it was not for any merit that others do not possess: not for power or wisdom at any rate. But you have been chosen, and you must therefore use such strength and heart and wits as you have.'

What is the Goal of the quest of the fellowship?

What is Sam's Final Goal?

What is Frodo's Final Goal?

You may ask "Why was I chosen?" And our Lord might reply..."You may be sure that it was
not for any merit that others do not possess: not for power or wisdom at any rate.
But you have been chosen! And you must therefore love and follow the Lord your God with all of your heart ,
and strength, and mind; and Love your neighbor as yourself as well."

What are some of the Final Goals of the quest of the fellowship of Believers?

What are Your Final Goals on your Spiritual Journey?

©2010, 2017. Wheaton Press™ All Rights Reserved.

The Fellowship of the Ring NOTES: The Quest "I will take it…"

The Council of Elrond at Rivendell:
>   *Book 2: Ch 1: "Many Meetings", Ch 2: "The council of Elrond"*

- *If they do not destroy the Ring it will eventually destroy them.* What are some "Rings In our world?
  - Family, School, Church, Community, Country, World…

- Borimir wants to use this evil yet powerful ring against the Enemy. His mistake here is a misunderstanding of evil. He thinks that he can use powerful evil tools and devices against a powerful evil enemy.

- Frodo Declares his willing heart when he states "I will take it!" What are some significant aspects of the Hobbit Volunteering?

Artwork courtesy of Princess Allison Spoelhof

 ©2010, 2017. Wheaton Press™ All Rights Reserved.

Myth: A Final Lesson – Life as Epic Adventure and Journey
Character connection: a way to dive deeper into "applicability"

Submit this written assignment as part of your philosophy final exam.

Paragraph #1:
    Pick a character in an epic tale that you connect with and describe what his or her gifts and talents are. What are at least three of his or her virtues (refer to the virtue list)? Give concrete examples from the text with page numbers where he or she displays these virtues.

Paragraph #2:
    Using creative analysis, explain how this character is valuable to the community of the tale in addition to how his or her character and virtues add to the group and the quest as a whole.

Paragraph #3:
    Using "mythical analysis," connect this character and his or her virtues to the True Myth – the True Biblical Story we are in. Find at least two biblical connections to these virtues and your character. Put the verse with the references in your paper.

Paragraph #4:
    Describe some of your own gifts and talents. What are some of your virtues (refer to the virtue list)? Give a concrete example of these virtues in action within the last year of your life. Describe the effect of these virtues on your quality of life and the quality of life for the others involved in your scenarios/examples.

Paragraph #5:
    Explain how your virtues are/can be an asset to the "Fellowship of Believers", the body of Christ, the Communion of the Saints. Use Scripture to explain how your virtues are Biblically based. Please put the verses and the references into your paper. Give a future example or goal of how you can/will strengthen the "Bride of Christ" on our quest together using these virtues, gifts, and talents.

Paragraph #6:
    Using synthesis and analysis with the curriculum from this semester: Describe, explain, and apply at least one concrete lesson from this quest and character assignment in the context of our study in philosophy and theology.

Myth: A Final Lesson – Life as Epic Adventure and Journey
Scripture Reading Integrity Assignments
Acts and "The True Myth"

Read and annotate the letter of Acts written by the Luke as a letter in one sitting. Pretend you are a member of the church. Where do you see connections to our discussions on the Quest and My Quest? The connections you make can be subtle, overt, literary, historical, artistic, personal, or metaphoric.

In the space below, write down at least three verses that you find engaging, and briefly explain why you picked these verses. Cut and paste or write out the entire verse, but do not simply put the reference. Do not summarize the verse as a response.

Photo Credits and Licensing!

The artwork and photos have been purchased or used with direct permission from the creator of the artwork or the photo; the name of the artist (or "istock") has been placed next to the piece. The exceptions to this are listed below, all of which have come from public use sites, particularly Yahoo and Google images under the licensing "Free to modify, share, and use commercially."

Aslan Picture #1:

https://images.search.yahoo.com/yhs/search;_ylt=AwrB8prGvOtXtUMAKFQunllQ?p=aslan&fr=yhs-mozilla-004&hsimp=yhs-004&hspart=mozilla&imgl=fmsuc&fr2=p%3As%2Cv%3Ai#id=3&iurl=http%3A%2F%2Fwww3.telus.net%2Fst_simons%2Faslan2.jpg&action=click & http://arend-mythologicalallusions.wikispaces.com/Film+Allusions

Lion Picture #2:

https://images.search.yahoo.com/yhs/ & https://upload.wikimedia.org/wikipedia/commons/1/13/Darica_Lion_07174.jpg

Magritte Picture "Treachery of Images"

https://images.search.yahoo.com/yhs/search;_ylt=AwrB8p9DxvNXcwYARu4unllQ?p=this+is+not+a+pipe+magritte&fr=yhs-mozilla-004&hsimp=yhs-004&hspart=mozilla&imgl=fmsuc&fr2=p%3As%2Cv%3Ai#id=2&iurl=http%3A%2F%2F4.bp.blogspot.com%2F-l3l1VKftxs8%2FUj7WcDsfSFl%2FAAAAAAAADkA%2FH_4SWd_Z_Bs%2Fs1600%2FBLOGNotaPipe.jpg&action=click & http://hellskitchennyc.blogspot.com/2013/09/this-is-not-pipe-previewing-magritte-at.html

- Thank you Jen Dominguez, Anna, Elijah, and Olivia for your artwork.

- Thank you Allison Spoelhof and Tim Burchfield for helping with design and drawings!

Artwork courtesy of Princess Allison Spoelhof

©2010, 2017. Wheaton Press™ All Rights Reserved.

Special Thanks!

This would literally not exist without the massive encouragement, support, expertise, and sacrifice of so many people the first of which is my wife and true friend Jennifer Dominguez. My children and dogs quickly fall in line after her. In an effort to honor everyone else who has helped I will definitely miss a few names but the attempt is still worthwhile; please forgive me if you were not mentioned here and should have been.

- Thank you Jen Dominguez for your Patient Perseverance and Commitment.
- Thank you Anna, Elijah, and Olivia for inspiring me each day!
- Thank you Chris Browne for being Batman!
- Thank you Charles Bressler for teaching me to love the power of metaphor and for introducing me to C. S. Lewis and the 4 world views in class and in Lewis' tour de force: "Miracles"
- Thank you Chris Grant for the inspiration, motivation, and the coffee, breakfasts, lunches…
- Thank you David Crowder, U2, Mumford and Sons, Rend Collective, The Brilliance, Josh Garrels, Hillsong United! and Bethel Worship…
- Thank you Bill Johnson Heidi Baker, Jon and Amy Gully, Kris Valliton, and Danny Silk, for teaching me how to listen to Him! His voice – has real authority and and real power.
- Thank you John Ortberg for "Walk on water" and Who is this man".
- Thank you Bob Goff for whimsy and "Love Does"
- Thank you Henri Nouwen for Return of the "Prodigal Son" & "Life of the Beloved"
- Thank you C.S. Lewis, G. K. Chesterton, and J. R. R. Tolkien everything but particularly for introducing me to the True Myth.
- Thank you to my many muses but particularly Jack Burgess & Nate Leman!
- Thank you for all of the feedback, pushback, and push forward to Scott Souders, Nick Le, Ben Varner, Micah Trautwein, Kole Maravilla, Tom Westervelt…
- Thank you to Sam Ruff for your editing and formatting prowess!
- Thank you Mark Hollingsworth and the students who gave this Thinkbook a test run in the Spring of 2016
- Thank you Trish Main, Jen Underwood, Margaret Becker, and so many other Wheaton Academy Teachers
- Thank you Matt Browning #Distinction and Eric Bowling #Monism.
- Thank you Tate Fritz for being Aragorn and Theoden.
- Thank you Paul Mouw and Linda Howard for believing in me on this Journey!
- Thank you Richard Rohr - for The BIG Vision and for Honor for a tone of relaxed Honor. For the Invitation. The Shalom. Thank you for teaching me how to die before I die. Thank you for teaching me about God in me, about union with The one true God. Thank you for permission to absolutely unashamedly boldly proudly deeply love paradox.
- Thank you Hafiz for showing me freedom, for inviting me to dance with The Friend, for showing me that Divine Union is the goal of spiritual formation.
- Thank you Darren Wilson for documenting your journey out a relationship with the Religious Spirit into a relationship with the Holy Spirit, particularly in your "Father of Lights" film. #Conviction & #Inspiration.
- Thank you Allison Spoelhof and Tim Burchfield for helping with design and drawings!

Enjoy the Journey.

Remember, you are Loved!

 ©2010, 2017. Wheaton Press™ All Rights Reserved.

22730047R00100

Made in the USA
Columbia, SC
31 July 2018